Diplomacy and Revolution

The
**FRANCO-AMERICAN
ALLIANCE *of* 1778**

Diplomacy and Revolution

The FRANCO-AMERICAN ALLIANCE *of* 1778

Edited by RONALD HOFFMAN
and PETER J. ALBERT

Published for the

UNITED STATES CAPITOL HISTORICAL SOCIETY

BY THE UNIVERSITY PRESS OF VIRGINIA

Charlottesville

THE UNIVERSITY PRESS OF VIRGINIA
Copyright © 1981 by the Rector and Visitors
of the University of Virginia

First published 1981

Library of Congress Cataloging in Publication Data
Main entry under title:
Diplomacy and revolution.
Includes index.
1. United States—Foreign relations—Revolution,
1775–1783—Addresses, essays, lectures. 2. United
States—History—Revolution, 1775–1783—French partici-
pation—Addresses, essays, lectures. I. Hoffman,
Ronald, 1941–   II. Albert, Peter J. III. United
States Capitol Historical Society, Washington, D.C.
E249.D5 973.3'2'4 80-13931 ISBN 0-8139-0864-7

Printed in the United States of America

CONTENTS

Preface

ON MAY 4, 1778, the Continental Congress of the United States ratified the two treaties that formed the Franco-American alliance. This action constituted the formal adoption of the separate accords pledging friendship and commerce and mutual defense which the American commissioners to the French government had negotiated on February 6, 1778. Both contemporaries and subsequent students of the American Revolution have recognized the crucial importance of these agreements to the survival of the young nation. As historian Samuel Flagg Bemis concluded in his extensive study *The Diplomacy of the American Revolution,* "The French Alliance was decisive for the cause of American independence." Similarly, David Ramsay, South Carolina patriot and one of the earliest historians of the Revolution and the early republic, assessed with unusual insight the motives for and the significance of the Franco-American alliance. Ramsay's analysis, contained in his *History of the United States,* published in 1816, provides an interesting and appropriate introduction to this series of essays.

At the close of his chapter entitled "The Alliance between France and the United States," Ramsay perceptively observed that Great Britain "had begun with *wrong* measures and had now got into *wrong* time." In retrospect, Ramsay might well have applied the same judgment to the French experience of the 1770s and 1780s. Only the United States, in his view, was in correct

vii

time in 1778. Ramsay's concept of time is central to his interpretation of the fortuitous nature of the Franco-American alliance for the new nation whose interests it served exceedingly well. By contrast, the economic burdens occasioned by the pact and the ideological enthusiasms it engendered proved to be ultimately disastrous for the French monarchy.

From Ramsay's perspective there was no doubt about what impelled nation-states to act. Measures were never taken out of "disinterested generosity." All the protagonists, he was convinced, proceeded in concert with "the known selfishness of human nature." Ramsay did not gainsay the importance of ideology, principle, and honor, but these were supplemental factors that invariably conformed to the goals of self-interest. From the beginning of the war, American objectives were clear: survival and independence. The French aim was equally obvious: the dismemberment of Great Britain's empire. Initially, France pursued her goal through a temporizing program of assistance calculated to expand the American revolt, thereby widening disruption within the British dominions. However, the Continental army's victory at Saratoga created a new context that demanded, as the French undoubtedly recognized, a different policy. Ramsay argued that the crushing defeat and capture of Burgoyne's army posed a clear danger to French interests; after Saratoga, the possibility of Britain's offering generous terms to secure a rapprochement with her former colonies became a live option. According to Ramsay's reasoning, Great Britain's strategy would be to resurrect her imperial dominance through the establishment of a firm Anglo-American alliance. France, by contrast, had to move quickly to frustrate any efforts in that direction. "Previous delay," Ramsay wrote, "had favored the dismemberment of the Empire; but further procrastination bid fair to promote at least such a federal alliance of the disjointed parts of the British Empire as would be no less hostile to the interests of France than a reunion of its several parts." Consequently, the French diplomat Conrad Alexandre Gérard wrote candidly to the American commissioners in Paris about his nation's desire to enter into an alliance. Gérard observed that it was "manifestly the interest of France that the power of England should be diminished, by the separation of its colonies from its government. The only condition he [the king] should require and rely on would be that the United States in no peace to be made should give up their independence and return to the obedience of the British government."

In this regard, France's policies succeeded admirably. Certainly one of the main reasons that the Continental Congress rejected the very generous and real concessions offered in 1778 by the new team of British commissioners led by the earl of Carlisle, involved the framework of mutual benefits, principle, and honor instituted by the alliance with France. In addition, as Ramsay notes, there lay at the bottom of Congress's refusal the impulse of self-interest. Carlisle and his colleagues had no chance; all human sensibilities conspired against them. "The leaders in Congress and the legislative assemblies of America," asserted Ramsay, "had tasted the sweets of power." To expect them now to relinquish such a prerogative was to defy "the passions of human nature."

The significance of the victory that produced the alliance also intrigued Ramsay, and he advanced an interesting and insightful analysis of it that subsequent historians have rarely explored. Ramsay noted that the capture of Burgoyne's army at Saratoga convinced the French that the Revolution was not simply the work of a few men who had seized power but the effort of a great body of people—an effort that was likely to be successful. Therefore, concluding an alliance with the young nation became for the French a viable and desirable policy. Similarly, in America the victory and the ensuing alliance enabled the Continental Congress, now that the potential for securing independence was a credible reality, to obtain for the first time majoritarian support for the war effort. Although Ramsay remained uncertain as to exactly when these shifts occurred, he considered the fall and winter of 1778–79 to have been decisive. He related that early in the war English opinion had maintained "that Congress was supported by a faction and that the great body of people was hostile to independence and well disposed to unite with Great Britain." The latter of these assertions, Ramsay continued, "was true till a certain period of the contest, but that period was elapsed." Such a perception of the domestic as well as the foreign impact of the alliance indicates that Ramsay perceived to some degree at least that aspect of the American Revolution suggested many years later by historian Carl L. Becker, who wrote in 1909 that the issues central to the War for Independence focused not only upon who should rule but upon who should rule at home.

Since the era of David Ramsay, historians have presented many additional perspectives to account for and interpret the Franco-American alliance of 1778. In the first essay in this volume Alexander DeConde contrasts the traditional historiography of the alliance with less conventional assessments. DeConde explores a number of specific topics relating to the alliance, such as the long-range motivations behind French policy between 1763 and 1778 and the more immediate factors that led to the agreement of 1778, its impact on the conduct of the war and on the making of the peace, and its significance both in the years following the Revolution and on American foreign policy in general.

William C. Stinchcombe examines American attitudes toward the alliance, using as his vantage points the celebrations in the autumn of 1781 and the summer of 1782 following the victory at Yorktown and the birth of the dauphin. Despite the paradox of an alliance between a revolutionary republic and an absolutist monarchy and the decades of hostility between the English colonists and the French in North America, the size and scope of these demonstrations, Stinchcombe argues, indicated the extent to which Americans accepted the treaties with France. In his view the celebrations marked the reaffirmation of American loyalty to the alliance and the acknowledgment of European influence in American affairs at the very time when the interests of the United States and France were growing increasingly divergent.

In contrast, Jonathan R. Dull and Orville T. Murphy discuss the alliance from the French perspective. Dull describes French intervention in the American Revolution as a tragedy for that nation, a misguided effort of men imprisoned by their situation and their limitations, culminating in bankruptcy and revolution for France. He traces France's declining role in the European balance of power and her diminishing capacity to influence European diplomacy and argues that these factors led her statesmen to intervene in the Revolution against Great Britain. It was the course of events in Europe, particularly the partition of Poland in 1772, that precipitated French intervention in America; similarly, the development of a crisis in the Crimea in 1782 led to its termination.

As a counterpoint to Dull's examination of the broader spectrum of European affairs in shaping French policy toward the American Revolution, Murphy focuses his attention on the perceptions of Charles Gravier, comte de Vergennes, the French secretary of state for foreign affairs from 1774 to 1787. Vergennes believed that France should act as the arbiter of European relations and the protector of the status quo and that she was prevented from doing so both by her own weakness and by British opposition. The American Revolution, in Vergennes's view, provided France with the opportunity to rearrange the balance of power in Europe by disrupting the British Empire and thereby weakening Great Britain. Murphy also portrays Vergennes's changing conceptions of American military potential as they were influenced by the reports of de Kalb, Bonvouloir, Gérard, La Luzerne, and others.

In the concluding essay, Lawrence S. Kaplan compares Franco-American relations during the course of two alliances—the Franco-American alliance of 1778 and the NATO alliance of 1949. After he has outlined the factors that led to the formulation of those treaties and discussed the perceptions of each of the two nations during the time that the agreements were in force, Kaplan speculates on the entangling nature of these alliances and their relative benefits to France and to the United States.

The essays in this volume were originally read at a symposium sponsored in 1978 by the United States Capitol Historical Society in cooperation with the United States Congress. That meeting was the first in a sequence of annual conferences to be held by the society in recognition of the nation's bicentennial. The authors of the papers have revised and expanded them for publication. Through the conduct of the symposia series and the subsequent publication of the proceedings, the officers of the United States Capitol Historical Society and especially its president, Mr. Fred Schwengel, hope to advance our understanding of the formative period of the history of the United States.

Diplomacy and Revolution

The
FRANCO-AMERICAN
ALLIANCE *of* 1778

ALEXANDER DECONDE

The French Alliance
in Historical Speculation

IN THE PAST two hundred years historians have created
a considerable literature pertaining to the Franco-
American alliance of 1778, viewed by some scholars,
such as Edmund S. Morgan, as "the greatest diplomatic
victory the United States has ever achieved."[1] This volume of scholarly activity is understandable because that
alliance, even when stripped of high-flying rhetoric,
holds a position of fundamental importance in the
founding of the American nation. The story of the
alliance is well known and the only areas of disagree-
ment among scholars concern facts that are hazy, motivation that is uncertain, or speculation that derives from
weak circumstantial data. This kind of conjecture that
departs from the standard version of a familiar subject
or brings aspects of it into question often enriches un-

[1] *The Birth of the Republic, 1763–89* (Chicago, 1956), p. 84. David
Schoenbrun, *Triumph in Paris: The Exploits of Benjamin Franklin* (New
York, 1976), pp. 177–78, attributes this "diplomatic victory as great
as any that would be won on the battlefield" to Franklin.

1

derstanding but arouses intense interest mainly among scholars.

What, we may ask, accounts for this lack of interest among nonspecialists in dissenting interpretations of major events or subjects? I believe, especially in the instance of the French alliance, that the weight of tradition, or essentially the success of historians who advance what has become the conventional interpretation of events, has obscured or overwhelmed the evaluations of dissenters. As a result, many nonspecialists interested in the subject take the conventional appraisal for granted, not realizing that it too, sound though it may be, employs speculative judgments. Since the past we praise or condemn, accept or reject, comes to us through the syntheses of historians, I think it appropriate to reflect on the highlights of the generally accepted history of the Franco-American alliance and to compare them with dissenting speculations. What follows is the gist of the conventional account of the origins of the alliance.

After defeating France and Spain in the Seven Years' War ending in 1763, Great Britain emerged as the world's preeminent imperial power. Accustomed to the acceptance of their own country as the most powerful and civilized on earth, French leaders felt such deep humiliation that they could not adjust to the reality of British ascendancy. They brooded and sought an opportunity to avenge the losses of 1763. Most prominent in working out this policy of revenge were two men who carried major responsibility for France's foreign affairs after the defeat in 1763, Etienne François, duc de Choiseul, and Charles Gravier, comte de Vergennes. They assumed that much of Britain's wealth and power came from trade with her North American colonies and that, if Britain were deprived of this fountain of wealth, her power would diminish. Both ministers sent agents to North America to foment rebellion in the colonies against British rule. Astute colonials understood well the objectives of French policy. "I fancy," Benjamin Franklin observed of France in 1767, "that intriguing nation would like very well to meddle on occasion, and blow up the coals between Britain and her colonies; but I hope we shall give them no opportunity."[2]

Americans finally did provide such an opportunity in 1775, when resistance to British measures burst into open conflict. Those rebel leaders who viewed their struggle in an international as well as a local context expected foreign assistance, especially from France. In November the Second Continental Congress established a Committee of Secret Correspondence, a kind of foreign office, to explore the possibilities of obtaining help from foreign nations. Early in March 1776 this committee decided to send an agent to Paris to solicit arms and to explore the possibility of an alliance. It chose Silas Deane, a businessman from Connecticut, to carry out this mission, explaining in his instructions that France was "the power whose friendship it would be fittest for us to obtain and cultivate."[3]

Before Deane set foot on French soil, Vergennes put in motion a plan to help the American rebels. Persuaded by the arguments of Vergennes and others, Louis XVI authorized the expenditure of one million livres, or several million dollars, in secret aid to Americans. The king took this step despite the risk of war with Britain and a financial system so weak that France

[2] Benjamin Franklin to William Franklin, Aug. 28, 1767, Leonard W. Labaree et al., eds., *The Papers of Benjamin Franklin*, 20 vols. (New Haven, 1956–76), 14:244.

[3] Committee of Secret Correspondence to Silas Deane, Mar. 3, 1776, Francis Wharton, ed., *Revolutionary Diplomatic Correspondence of the United States*, 6 vols. (Washington, D.C., 1889), 2:79.

courted bankruptcy.[4] Six weeks later Charles III, king of Spain, put up an equivalent sum to support the Revolution. In August a fictitious trading company, *Rodrigue Hortalez et Cie,* funded by the Bourbon monarchs and headed by the playwright, adventurer, and diplomatic agent Caron de Beaumarchais, began supplying American fighters with money, guns, and munitions.

Simultaneously, American leaders decided that they needed more than secret aid. They assumed they could elicit more because Vergennes and other French statesmen were so eager to see England humbled that they would not hesitate to commit France to the American cause even without a reciprocal obligation. These Americans also considered the potential flow of commerce to and from North America to be so valuable it would give them considerable leverage in bargaining with France. Consequently, they believed that the French would be content to help disrupt Britain's empire and destroy her trade in North America without exacting a heavy price beforehand. Later, France would be grateful for an opportunity to take over that commerce for herself. Thomas Paine's pamphlet of January 1776, *Common Sense,* gave considerable publicity to this design. He called not only for independence but also for foreign assistance without political strings attached to it.

Other Americans felt that they could not attract large-scale French help without an alliance and that they must

---

[4] The status of French finances is beyond the scope of this essay, but it is a matter of speculation. The conventional analysis maintains that if France had not made the alliance with the United States and bankrupted herself, there would have been no French Revolution. See Jonathan R. Dull, *The French Navy and American Independence: A Study of Arms and Diplomacy, 1774–1787* (Princeton, 1975), p. 344; and Robert D. Harris, "French Finances and the American War, 1777–1783," *Journal of Modern History* 48 (1976): 233–58, which presents a dissenting analysis.

declare independence as a means of obtaining it. "It is not choice then, but necessity," Richard Henry Lee of Virginia wrote, "that calls for Independence, as the only means by which foreign Alliance can be obtained."[5] On June 7 he offered a resolution in Congress calling for independence, confederation, and "foreign alliances." Four days later Congress appointed a committee to draft a declaration of independence, and on the next day created another committee to prepare a plan of treaties to be proposed to foreign powers. This latter committee presented Congress with a plan and the model of a treaty, drafted by John Adams, to be submitted to France. That model called for a commercial agreement containing no political commitment from the United States.

At this point Adams and other revolutionaries did not necessarily construe the word *alliance* to mean a military obligation. They sometimes used the term *commercial alliance* as the equivalent of a trade agreement. "I am not for soliciting any political connection," Adams wrote privately, "or military assistance, or indeed naval, from France. I wish for nothing but commerce, a mere marine treaty with them."[6] Congress adopted the committee's plan, after making amendments, on September 17, 1776.

Nine days later Congress appointed three commissioners to negotiate agreements with European nations according to the principles of the Model Treaty. "It is

[5] Richard Henry Lee to Landon Carter, June 2, 1776, in James C. Ballagh, ed., *The Letters of Richard Henry Lee,* 2 vols. (New York, 1911), 1:198.

[6] John Adams to John Winthrop, June 23, 1776, in Charles Francis Adams, ed., *The Works of John Adams . . . ,* 10 vols. (Boston, 1850–56), 9:409. For ambiguities in the use of *alliance,* see Felix Gilbert, "The New Diplomacy of the Eighteenth Century," *World Politics* 4 (1951): 19–20.

highly probable," their instructions read, "that France means not to let the United States sink in the present Contest."[7] The most prominent of the commissioners, seventy-year-old Benjamin Franklin, landed in France early in December. Although received cordially, the American emissaries in Paris failed to secure either recognition of the United States or more aid. Since at the same time the war was going badly for Americans, Congress put aside fears of a political connection and sent new instructions to its agents in France authorizing them to secure military alliances with that country and with Spain.

Even though Vergennes and other officials desired such an alliance, they hesitated since a treaty would mean war with a Britain which still commanded the seas and which still retained the loyalty of many in North America. If France did not move cautiously, she might repeat the disaster of the Seven Years' War. She "feared lest the colonists might all at once desist, and resume all their ancient relations with England."[8] Vergennes decided to wait until Americans demonstrated not only a will to fight but also the skill to do so successfully and an ability to remain independent of Britain over the long pull.

The need for waiting ended early in December 1777, when Vergennes learned the results of Saratoga. There, on October 17, a British army under the command of Gen. John Burgoyne capitulated to American forces under Gen. Horatio Gates. This news, along with information that the British were now willing to offer conces-

[7] Instructions to the Agent, Sept. 24, 1776, in Gilbert Chinard, ed., *The Treaties of 1778 and Allied Documents* (Baltimore, 1928), p. 17.

[8] Carlo G. G. Botta, *History of the War of the Independence of the United States of America,* trans. Alexander Otis, 6th ed. rev. 2 vols. (New Haven, 1834), 2:77. Botta's analysis of French motivation is sophisticated and thorough.

sions that Americans might accept, persuaded the French to proceed with the alliance which Americans desired. Otherwise Americans might end their Revolution and return to the British Empire.

The British, understandably, tried to defeat the alliance. Through special agents in Paris, Lord North, head of the British government, attempted several times in December 1777 and January 1778 to obtain terms for a reconciliation from Franklin. One agent said that the British government was now willing to grant Americans everything they might ask "except the word *independence*."[9] North's agents also reminded Americans that they had nothing in common with the French. As in the past, loyalists insisted, France remained America's natural enemy rather than friend. These tactics failed.

On February 6, 1778, representatives of France and the United States signed three agreements in Paris. In the first, a treaty of amity and commerce, France formally recognized the United States as an independent country. In return, Americans promised special trading privileges that were potentially valuable. The second document, a treaty of alliance, provided that when Britain responded to France's recognition with war, the new allies would fight together in "common cause." Each pledged to conclude neither truce nor peace with Britain "without the formal consent of the other first obtained."[10] France promised, as her prime purpose, to wage war until American independence was assured. She also renounced claim to territory in North America

[9] James Hutton, quoted in Weldon A. Brown, *Empire or Independence: A Study in the Failure of Reconciliation, 1774–1783* (1941; reprint ed., Baton Rouge, La., 1966), p. 208.

[10] The quotations are from articles I and VIII of the alliance. See Chinard, *Treaties of 1778*, pp. 52 and 54.

that she had lost in 1763. In exchange, the United States said it would defend French possessions in the Caribbean. The term of the alliance was "forever." The third instrument, held secret, reserved a place for Spain in the alliance.

Dissenters challenge several aspects of the conventional account up to this point, usually focusing on the motivation of the French in making the alliance. Regardless of how skilled, historians cannot pinpoint what actuates a nation. Often, however, they can ascertain what drives those who have the power to make decisions. From this knowledge scholars can speculate broadly on why a nation or government behaved in a particular manner. Even with such evidence, knowledge cannot be precise, mainly because historians generally use selective personal data—letters, diaries, and statements—from those few people in positions of power whose documents survive, or are accessible, for wide-ranging conjectures.

Such data support the conventional theory that French leaders could not ignore the splendid opportunity presented by the American Revolution to avenge the losses of 1763. They desired the alliance as the instrument of their revenge.[11] Critics of this thesis

[11] The revenge theory is so widespread that it can be found in numerous books and articles. For a discussion of the theory see Ramon E. Abarca, "Classical Diplomacy and Bourbon 'Revanche' Strategy, 1763–1770," *Review of Politics* 32 (1970): 313–37. For analyses of French motivation, see Edward S. Corwin, "The French Objective in the American Revolution," *American Historical Review* 21 (1915): 33–61; Arthur B. Darling, *Our Rising Empire, 1763–1803* (New Haven, 1940), pp. 22–26; and Don Higginbotham, *The War of American Independence: Military Attitudes, Policies, and Politics, 1763–1789* (New York, 1971), pp. 230–32, and especially note 12, pp. 252–53. For expressions of the revenge theory, see Henri Doniol, *Histoire de la participation de la France à l'établissement des Etats-Unis d'Amérique*, 5 vols. (Paris, 1886–92), 1:4; Samuel Flagg Bemis, *The Diplomacy of the American Revolution*, 2d ed. (1935; reprint ed., Bloomington, Ind., 1957), p. 16; Richard W. Van Alstyne, *Empire*

argue from various perspectives, but they have in common the general idea that nations do not shape policy to gratify the emotion of anger or inflict injury on other countries merely to be vindictive, as revenge implies. In addition to revenge, or in place of it, theories of motivation emphasize such factors as desire for power in Europe, national survival, territory in North America, response to alleged popular support for liberal ideas, and hope for commercial advantage.

Most persuasive is the hypothesis advanced by Edward S. Corwin and others, maintaining that France entered the alliance for reasons of prestige and power. Her leaders, notably Choiseul and Vergennes, wished to weaken England, create a new balance of power in Europe, and restore France to her former greatness.[12] They expected war, and planned for it, to attain this

---

and Independence: The International History of the American Revolution (New York, 1966), p. 47, questions the theory while accepting it; Lawrence S. Kaplan, *Colonies into Nation: American Diplomacy, 1763–1801* (New York, 1972), p. 111; René de la Croix, duc de Castries, *La France et l'Indépendance américaine: Le livre du bicentenaire de l'Indépendance* (Paris, 1975), pp. 107 and 345; and R. John Singh, *French Diplomacy in the Caribbean and the American Revolution* (Hicksville, N.Y., 1977), where the theory is repeated throughout the book.

[12] See Edward S. Corwin, *French Policy and the American Alliance of 1778* (Princeton, 1916), pp. v, 16, 18, 22, 49, and 51; Ben C. McCary, *The Causes of the French Intervention in the American Revolution* (Toulouse, 1928), pp. 165, 210, and 214; John J. Meng, *The Comte de Vergennes: European Phases of His American Diplomacy (1774–1780)* (Washington, D.C., 1932), pp. 10 and 64; John F. Ramsey, *Anglo-French Relations, 1763–1770: A Study of Choiseul's Foreign Policy* (Berkeley, Calif., 1939), pp. 164–66, which does not mention the revenge theory; Max Savelle, "The American Balance of Power and European Diplomacy, 1713–78," in Richard B. Morris, ed., *The Era of the American Revolution* (New York, 1939), pp. 162, 164, and 166; Gerald Stourzh, *Benjamin Franklin and American Foreign Policy* (Chicago, 1954), pp. 137–39; and Orville T. Murphy, "Charles Gravier de Vergennes: Portrait of an Old Regime Diplomat," *Political Science Quarterly* 83 (1968): 402–3.

goal. Not all French leaders accepted such reasoning. Louis XVI's minister of finance, Anne Robert Jacques Turgot, for instance, argued that an alliance risked too much for too little. France's finances could not sustain a war with Britain. In time, moreover, Britain would lose her colonies and her empire would collapse. Turgot concluded, therefore, that Americans did not need French help to achieve independence, and France did not require war to enhance her power.

A counterspeculation, put forth by Henri Doniol and Claude H. Van Tyne, suggests that Vergennes sought something more basic than power or prestige. This theory states that he feared a reconciliation between England and her colonies that would revive their long-shared animosities against France. Then the Anglo-American coalition would strike at French and Spanish possessions in the Caribbean, and perhaps at France herself. This concern persuaded the French crown not to wait until the English allies struck, but to intervene openly in North America and to accept the American alliance as an instrument for survival.[13]

For a time a hypothesis articulated by Frederick Jackson Turner and repeated by others gained favor among professional historians. It denied any defensive self-interest in French motivation. Even though in the alliance France disclaimed territorial ambitions in North America, this theory goes, her disclaimer should not be taken at face value. She intended to use the alliance to rebuild her empire in North America, essentially through recovery of Canada and Louisiana. This inter-

[13] See Doniol, *Histoire,* 1:127 and 369; Claude H. Van Tyne, "Influences Which Determined the French Government to Make the Treaty with America, 1778," *American Historical Review* 21 (1916): 528–41; and Corwin, *French Policy and Alliance,* pp. 144–47, which criticizes Van Tyne's theory.

pretation, stressing imperial greed, rests on dubious or discredited evidence.[14]

Shaky, too, is support for the more romantic thesis of George Bancroft and Bernard Faÿ, which holds that "the movement of intellectual freedom" within French society produced the alliance. According to Carl L. Becker, French public opinion, imbued with "a spirit of liberal ideals," compelled Louis XVI to enter the treaties of 1778; what he and his ministers sought "above all" was "of a moral and intellectual nature." Critics of these ideas point out that French enthusiasm for the alliance came not from the people or from Paris salons but from the foreign office. It stemmed much less from any concern for American liberty than from enmity toward Britain.[15]

[14] Frederick Jackson Turner, "The Policy of France toward the Mississippi Valley in the Period of Washington and Adams," *American Historical Review* 10 (1905): 250–55; and Samuel Eliot Morison, *Life and Letters of Harrison Gray Otis, Federalist, 1765–1848*, 2 vols. (Boston, 1913), 1:66. For a critique of this theory or contrary evidence, see Corwin, *French Policy and Alliance*, pp. 9–11; John J. Meng, "The Place of Canada in French Diplomacy of the American Revolution," *Bulletin des Recherches Historiques* 29 (1939): 665–87. Gustave Lanctot, *Canada and the American Revolution, 1774–1783*, trans. Margaret M. Cameron (Toronto, 1967), p. 179, maintains that "public opinion in France . . . was deeply interested in the idea of a possible reconquest of Canada."

[15] See George Bancroft, *History of the United States of America, from the Discovery of the Continent*, 6 vols. (New York, 1896, author's last revision), 5:256 and 258; and Bernard Faÿ, *The Revolutionary Spirit in France and America . . .* , trans. Ramon Guthrie (New York, 1927), p. 104. For emphasis on the alleged impact of French public opinion, see Lewis Rosenthal, *America and France: The Influence of the United States on France in the Eighteenth Century* (New York, 1882), pp. 50, 54, and 55; and Carl L. Becker, *The Declaration of Independence: A Study in the History of Political Ideas* (1922; reprint ed., New York, 1959), p. 230, who writes that the French people approved of the alliance "with unbounded enthusiasm." For criticism see Corwin, *French Pol-*

More evidence may be found for another thesis. It maintains that France sought commercial rather than territorial rewards from the alliance. An independent United States would be grateful for help and would reward France by making her its foremost trading partner. France would capture the rich North American market that England would lose. Since this idea found expression in Congress's Model Treaty and in the writings of various Revolutionary leaders, it appeals to a number of scholars. A variation of this view holds that France took on the alliance and the war it brought with the purpose of breaking down British trade.[16] As the varying interpretations indicate, historians still differ as to the nature of French motivation, but few who investigate the subject in depth seem satisfied with the conventional revenge thesis.

Yet this concern with motivation, especially with revenge, leads readily to the theory that Frenchmen, not Americans, took the initiative in drawing up the alliance. Some writers suggest that France desired war with England and hence from the beginning of her secret aid she looked forward to an alliance. It was, according to an early expression of this concept by David Ramsay in 1789, France's "true policy" to intervene in North America "by degrees" and build a solid foundation for an alliance.[17] From the start of the Revolution her min-

icy and Alliance, p. 2; and Frances Acomb, *Anglophobia in France, 1763–1789: An Essay in the History of Constitutionalism and Nationalism* (Durham, N.C., 1950), pp. 72–73.

[16] Richard B. Morris, *The Peacemakers: The Great Powers and American Independence* (New York, 1965), p. 14; Durand Echeverria, *Mirage in the West: A History of the French Image of American Society to 1815* (Princeton, 1957), pp. 42 and 130; and Echeverria, ed., "Condorcet's *The Influence of the American Revolution on Europe*," *William and Mary Quarterly*, 3d ser. 25 (1968): 98.

[17] Quoted from David Ramsay, *The History of the American Revolution*, 2 vols. (1789; reprint ed., London, 1793), 2:60. See also John J.

isters indicated that if the American colonies declared independence, France would help them maintain it. Supporters of this thesis further assert that Americans really had no desire for a military and political connection, fearing it would make the United States a client state of France. They show how opponents of independence, exploiting distrust of France as an old enemy of Protestant Americans, used this argument. John Dickinson, for example, a popular Revolutionary pamphleteer who opposed independence, said that even if Americans should defeat Britain, "France must rise on her Ruins. Her Ambition. Her Religion. Our Dangers from thence. We shall weep at our Victory." [18]

This wariness toward France was exemplified both by the Model Treaty and also by the attitude of insurgent leaders in Congress.who wanted only a commercial connection. They disliked the idea of an alliance because it would tie the United States to French policy like a tail on a kite and endanger long-range American goals in foreign policy. Americans accepted the entangling connection because France demanded it as the price to be paid for increased support. The men of the Revolution had no choice, this interpretation asserts; they had to conclude the alliance to survive. "What is astounding," Felix Gilbert writes, "is how little the Americans were willing to offer." [19]

Meng, ed., *Dispatches and Instructions of Conrad Alexandre Gérard, 1778–1780* (Baltimore, 1939), p. 63.

[18] July 1, 1776, quoted in James H. Hutson, "Intellectual Foundations of Early American Diplomacy," *Diplomatic History* 1 (1977): 15.

[19] The quotation comes from Felix Gilbert, *To the Farewell Address: Ideas of Early American Foreign Policy* (Princeton, 1961), p. 53. See also Darling, *Our Rising Empire*, p. 2; Brown, *Empire or Independence*, p. 170; Stourzh, *Benjamin Franklin*, pp. 132 and 137; and Gregg L. Lint, "The Law of Nations and the American Revolution," in Law-

The conventional view insists, however, that Americans, rather than Frenchmen, made the initial overtures, that they declared independence mainly to attract an alliance, and, according to John J. Meng, that "they offered France *carte blanche* in drawing up the terms of the alliance for which they were pleading."[20] It states that American arms could not cope with British military power. When insurgent leaders realized that commercial incentives, as in the terms of the Model Treaty, would not bring immediate French recognition, they pressed for a military agreement. Americans needed foreign aid in any form but desired a firm and sustained commitment to their cause, as in a treaty of alliance, and that is what their representatives in France and Spain sought.[21]

In support of this conventional analysis, expressed most recently and cogently by Lawrence S. Kaplan, scholars point out that Benjamin Franklin used the possibility of a reconciliation with England to goad the French into an alliance. In January 1778 he told Conrad Alexandre Gérard, chief assistant to Vergennes, that

rence S. Kaplan, ed., *The American Revolution and "A Candid World"* (Kent, Ohio, 1977), p. 115.

[20] The quotation comes from Meng, "Canada in French Diplomacy," p. 67. For a revisionist analysis that argues Congress resolved on independence mainly because it feared that Britain would partition North America with France and Spain in exchange for their help in suppressing the rebellion, see James H. Hutson, "The Partition Treaty and the Declaration of American Independence," *Journal of American History* 58 (1972): especially 877 and 896.

[21] See, for example, Kaplan, *Colonies into Nation*, pp. 112 and 114; idem, "Toward Isolationism: The Rise and Fall of the Franco-American Alliance, 1775–1801," in Kaplan, *American Revolution*, p. 138; William C. Stinchcombe, "John Adams and the Model Treaty," ibid., pp. 71 and 74–75; idem, *The American Revolution and the French Alliance* (Syracuse, N.Y., 1969); and Richard W. Van Alstyne, *The Rising American Empire* (New York, 1960), pp. 34–35.

only "the immediate conclusion of a treaty of commerce and alliance" would close American ears to any English proposal short of full independence. When Gérard responded that France would comply as soon as Americans wished, Franklin apparently reacted with surprise. He "observed that this was what they [the American commissioners] had proposed and solicited vainly for a year past."[22]

This argument in favor of American initiative seems particularly convincing when linked to the impact of Saratoga. According to the conventional synthesis, Franklin succeeded finally in gaining French adherence to an alliance because shortly before conferring with Gérard news of the American victory at Saratoga had reached Paris. John Adams, as well as other contemporaries, was convinced that "it determined the wavering counsels of France to an alliance." In this view the Battle of Saratoga marked a major turning point in the American Revolution. It signaled the beginning of warfare by Europeans against England in various parts of the globe and hence, in the view of Samuel Flagg Bemis, a distinguished scholar of this period, might well "be ranked among the 'fifteen decisive battles of the world.' "[23]

[22] These are Gérard's words recalling Franklin's conversation, quoted in Stourzh, *Benjamin Franklin*, p. 140. See also James B. Perkins, *France in the American Revolution* (Boston, 1911), p. 239, with comments on the alliance as a pact between equals; and Samuel Flagg Bemis, "British Secret Service and the French-American Alliance," *American Historical Review* 29 (1924): 488–89.

[23] The first quotation comes from Adams, *Works of John Adams*, 1:271, and the second from Bemis, *Diplomacy of the American Revolution*, p. 61. Bemis obtained this phrase from Edward S. Creasy, *The Fifteen Decisive Battles of the World from Marathon to Waterloo* (1851; reprint ed., London, 1915). For other expressions of this view, see Max B. May, *France: Her Influence and Aid in Our Revolutionary Struggle*, University of Cincinnati, 2d ser., Bulletin no. 17 (Cincinnati, 1902), p. 12; Doniol, *Histoire*, 2:610–67; Claude H. Van Tyne,

Those who dissent from this orthodoxy do not agree on a single alternative analysis. A British historian, J. H. Plumb, suggests that England's general inability to crush the American rebels convinced the French they must make the alliance and intervene openly.[24] Richard W. Van Alstyne, an American diplomatic historian, also minimizes the importance of Saratoga. He focuses on naval activity in the Caribbean. His thesis maintains that in the summer of 1777 France had to accept war with England or retreat, once again in humiliation, from her program of aid to Americans. The time of decision, according to this assessment, came early in September 1777, while Burgoyne's army was still marching south. By that time a British blockade in the Caribbean threatened to throttle the United States economically. In desperation American leaders pleaded for French and Spanish naval intervention to break the blockade. Since France wanted to avoid an American defeat followed by reconciliation with Britain, she went ahead with the alliance. Her leaders, this conjecture holds, believed that their aid to Americans would lead inevitably to a clash with the British in the Caribbean, so why not choose a time that seemed favorable?[25]

"French Aid before the Alliance of 1778," *American Historical Review* 21 (1925): 40; William Gordon, *The History of the Rise, Progress and Establishment of Independence of the United States of America . . .* , 4 vols. (London, 1788), 3:96; Helen Augur, *The Secret War of Independence* (New York, 1955), p. 251; Piers Mackesy, *The War for America, 1775–1783* (Cambridge, Mass., 1964), p. 147; Jacques L. Godechot, *France and the Atlantic Revolution of the Eighteenth Century, 1770–1799,* trans. Herbert H. Rowen (New York, 1965), p. 33; and Castries, *La France et l'Indépendance américaine,* pp. 175 and 347.

[24] "The French Connection: The Alliance That Won the Revolution," *American Heritage* 26 (1974): 4. For another revisionist view, see Orville T. Murphy, "The Battle of Germantown and the Franco-American Alliance of 1778," *Pennsylvania Magazine of History and Biography* 82 (1958): 55–64.

[25] See Van Alstyne, *Empire and Independence,* pp. 132–33.

Jonathan R. Dull's revisionist appraisal of Saratoga also pivots on naval strategy. It suggests that French leaders had decided on war by the end of July 1777. Realizing that an alliance with the Americans would precipitate war, they held back until they could rebuild France's navy to a strength that would permit a serious challenge to Britain. According to this hypothesis, workers in France's dockyards, more than the outcome of a battle, or battles, in North America, influenced the timing of France's decision to replace limited involvement with full-scale intervention.[26]

This intervention, as told in the conventional narrative, developed just about as the French had planned. On March 13, 1778, the French ambassador in London informed the British government of what it already knew, that his country had recognized the United States. Four days later England reacted to this provoking announcement with a declaration of war on France. The French government drew up plans for an invasion of England.[27] Across the Atlantic on May 4 the Continental Congress, meeting in York, Pennsylvania, spurned British overtures for reconciliation and voted unanimous approval of the French treaties. Hostilities between the great powers began on June 17 when two British warships attacked a French frigate in the English Channel.

At last, as Americans had hoped and assumed it would, the French alliance transformed their Revolution from a local uprising into a key element in an international war. Later, Spain and the Netherlands also fought against England. France sent armies and fleets to North America, subsidized the United States government with loans and gifts, and braced a sagging econ-

[26] Dull, *French Navy and American Independence,* pp. 89–94.

[27] See A. Temple Patterson, *The Other Armada: The Franco-Spanish Attempt to Invade Britain in 1779* (Manchester, 1960), pp. 13–14.

omy. American soldiers carried muskets made in France, fired French cannon, and received pay from French sources. France also provided the naval and military superiority at the siege of Yorktown that forced surrender of Gen. Charles Cornwallis's army on October 19, 1781, and that brought victory to the allies in North America.

In this victory as in the general achievement of American independence, the alliance proved the essential element or "deciding factor." Diplomatic historians appear to consider this judgment virtually as dogma; few depart from it. Without the alliance, they say, the Revolution would have failed, since "without France the Americans were completely helpless."[28]

Dissent comes mainly from military and political historians. Their speculation, however, has had little influence on the writings of conventional diplomatic historians. Military historians give more credit to the fighting ability of Americans than to diplomacy for the victory over Britain. John R. Alden writes, for example, that "if one sets aside intervention by God or by Fate, if one does not inflate the strength of the British state, it will appear that the Patriots did not struggle against overwhelming odds. It is even quite possible that they would have gained independence without the help of the French—and Spanish—armies and navies."[29] Even

[28] See Bemis, *Diplomacy of the American Revolution,* pp. vii–viii, 86, and 255; Corwin, *French Policy and Alliance,* p. 358; Van Alstyne, *Empire and Independence,* p. 200; Stinchcombe, *American Revolution and French Alliance,* pp. 152 and 212; Henry Blumenthal, *France and the United States: Their Diplomatic Relations, 1789–1914* (Chapel Hill, N.C., 1970), pp. 4–5; William A. Williams, *Contours of American History* (1961; reprint ed., Chicago, 1966), p. 120; and Ralph L. Ketcham, "France and American Politics, 1763–1793," *Political Science Quarterly* 78 (1963), p. 198.

[29] *A History of the American Revolution* (New York, 1969), p. 245. See also Higginbotham, *War of American Independence,* pp. 431–32.

in dark hours, these interpreters argue, the American will to resist British subjugation remained evident. They find such determination in the sentiments of prominent rebels. In the autumn of 1777 Franklin, for instance, maintained that "we shall derive Resources from our Distress, like the Earth-born Giant Antaeus, who derived new Strength from his Falls."[30]

Piers Mackesy, a British scholar, writes that Americans might have persisted in hit-and-run tactics and guerrilla warfare "indefinitely till Britain tired of the contest and withdrew from a country she could not govern." Even some French officers in North America, who often despaired over George Washington's regulars, acknowledged the importance of American opposition. "No opinion was clearer," one of them observed in retrospect, "than that though the people of America might be conquered by well disciplined European troops, the country of America was unconquerable." Long before his defeat at Yorktown Lord Cornwallis, too, repeatedly said the conquest of the American rebels was impracticable.[31]

Other military and political historians assert that the outcome of the war in North America, as in all military conflicts, hinged not on one battle or a single treaty but

[30] W. Carmichael, quoting Franklin to Tourville, Nov. 1, 1777, quoted in Stourzh, *Benjamin Franklin*, p. 135. Others, even in distant Russia, assumed by 1778 that Americans were gaining freedom on their own. See Nikolai Bolkhovitinov, *The Beginnings of Russian-American Relations, 1775–1815*, trans. Elena Levin (Cambridge, Mass., 1975), p. 8.

[31] Quotations are from Mackesy, *War for America*, pp. 510 and 511. See also Robert R. Palmer, *The Age of Democratic Revolution: A Political History of Europe and America, 1760–1800*, vol. 1, *The Challenge* (Princeton, 1959), pp. 209–10; and Don Higginbotham, "American Historians and the Military History of the American Revolution," *American Historical Review* 70 (1964): 32. For Cornwallis, see Solomon Lutnick, *The American Revolution and the British Press, 1775–1783* (Columbia, Mo., 1967), p. 193.

on a complex relationship of strategy, economics, and diplomacy. Although powerful, the British navy, for example, was not strong enough to guard the Channel coast against a possible French and Spanish attack and at the same time wage effective war against Americans. Nor, according to this analysis by David Syrett, could England's navy mount a blockade sufficiently effective to prevent munitions from reaching American armies. The flow of arms from abroad, along with the inability of British troops to inflict decisive defeat on Washington's forces, indicated that Americans could wage war indefinitely. Even with the help of the navy, military theorists suggest, British forces in North America were too few to subjugate Americans.[32]

Another related theory, but one which has dubious validity, holds "that American colonists were fully able to conduct the contest against England alone" except for British use of mercenary troops such as Hessians. Otherwise "America would have triumphed single-handed in the war of independence. . . . It was the employment of these foreign soldiers which compelled the patriots to seek" the alliance.[33]

Military historians say little about the alliance and peacemaking. Conventional diplomatic historians, while

[32] See David Syrett, "Defeat at Sea: The Impact of American Naval Operations upon the British, 1775–1778," Department of the Navy, Naval History Division, *Maritime Dimensions of the American Revolution* (Washington, D.C., 1977), pp. 13, 16, and 20; and Charles Stedman, *The History of the Origin, Progress, and Termination of the American War,* 2 vols. (Dublin, 1794), 2:502. For exaggerated speculation on the importance of the naval activity, see Edgar S. Maclay, *A History of American Privateers* (New York, 1899), p. xi. See also James A. Woodburn, "France and the American Revolution," *Chautauqua* 25 (1897): 251; Marshall Smelser, "An Understanding of the American Revolution," *Review of Politics* 38 (1976): 307.

[33] Richard H. Clark, "France's Aid to America in the War of Independence," *American Catholic Quarterly Review* 22 (1897): 408.

considering the alliance indispensable in winning the war, view it as an obstacle to American interests in the making of peace. Under French pressure, their narrative goes, Congress instructed its peace commissioners to govern themselves by strict adherence to the alliance. They were "to undertake nothing in the negotiations for peace or truce" without French knowledge or concurrence.[34] Two of the peace commissioners, John Adams and John Jay, discerned that France placed the interests of Spain, her other ally, ahead of obligations to the United States. Spain wished to prolong the war until she and France could wrench Gibraltar from England. In North America, Spain wished to acquire territory east of the Mississippi River, desired by Americans, and thereby confine the United States to the Atlantic seaboard. When the British expressed willingness to grant peace and independence on generous terms, therefore, the American commissioners ignored their instructions and engaged in secret negotiations on their own with British representatives. On November 30, 1782, without consulting or informing the French, they signed provisional articles of peace with Britain.

Reflecting a patriotic bias, the conventional interpreters of these events advance essentially a conspiracy thesis. In the view of Jonathan R. Dull "the traditional American account of these negotiations resembles a kind of Yankee morality play."[35] In the peace negotiations, traditionalists say, French leaders "deceived" and "betrayed" the United States and sought to manipulate American commissioners as though they were puppets.[36]

[34] Samuel Huntington, Instructions to Commissioners, June 15, 1781, Wharton, *Revolutionary Diplomatic Correspondence,* 4:505.

[35] Dull, *French Navy and American Independence,* p. 326.

[36] See Morris, *Peacemakers,* p. 459, who depicts the peacemaking as an encounter between European guile, mainly French and Spanish,

When, for example, the British negotiator Richard Oswald noted that the American commissioners were fearful "of being made the tools of the powers of Europe," John Adams replied, "Indeed I am." Then Adams added, "It is obvious that all the powers of Europe will be continually manœuvring with us, to work us into their real or imaginary balances of power. They will all wish to make of us a make-weight candle."[37]

Essentially, Adams and John Jay distrusted Vergennes, believing he wanted to prevent the United States from acquiring the trans-Appalachian west and to deny Americans access to fisheries off Newfoundland. Jay believed of the French, "it is not their interest that we should become a great and formidable people, and therefore they will not help us become so."[38] Adams concurred in this view. "When we see the French intriguing with the English against us," he wrote, "we have no way to oppose it but by reasoning with the English to show that they are intended to be the dupes."[39]

and American innocence, with Americans acquiring needed sophistication; Kaplan, *Colonies into Nation,* pp. 134, 140, and 144; Stinchcombe, *American Revolution and French Alliance,* p. 190, who shows American distrust of France and Spain; and Bemis, *Diplomacy of the American Revolution,* p. 187, who says at an earlier juncture that France "would have tricked the United States out of its independence." Some writers also blame French duplicity for the failure of an American mission by Francis Dana to St. Petersburg. See David M. Griffiths, "American Commercial Diplomacy in Russia, 1780 and 1783," *William and Mary Quarterly,* 3d ser. 27 (1970): 379–80 and 401.

[37] The Adams and Oswald quotations come from Adams, *Works of John Adams,* diary entry of Nov. 18, 1782, 3:316.

[38] Jay's words are from Jay to Robert R. Livingston, Nov. 17, 1782, Henry P. Johnston, ed., *The Correspondence and Public Papers of John Jay,* 4 vols. (New York, 1890–93), 2:450.

[39] John Adams to Jonathan Jackson, Nov. 17, 1782, Adams, *Works of John Adams,* 9:517.

A minority of scholars, among them John J. Meng and Orville T. Murphy, discern no deception or plot against American interests. They point out that under the alliance there could be no peace without independence, and hence the alliance forced Britain to negotiate with the idea of recognizing an independent United States. In addition, they maintain that, while the alliance guaranteed American independence, it did not delineate the boundaries of the new nation and did not obligate France to fight either for American expansion beyond the Appalachians or for fishing privileges Americans desired but could not gain on their own. Nor do these interpreters perceive Vergennes as underhanded.[40] After all, his first duty was to France, and he could be expected, if he thought it necessary, to exact concessions from Americans if in doing so he advanced the interests of the French state. He could not, however, be expected knowingly to injure his own country, which was staggering from the financial strain of the war, so that Americans could achieve all that they desired or assumed should be theirs under the terms of the alliance. National self-interest functioned in about the same way for Frenchmen as for Americans.

This concept of betrayal has led some nationalistic purveyors of conventional history to admit that American peace commissioners violated the terms of the alliance in negotiating a separate peace treaty secretly, but to argue that French deceit justified their procedure. Most scholars, however, appraise as proper the action of American negotiators in breaking with their instructions and with French control. In so doing the commissioners did not, according to conventional nationalists,

[40] See Ramsay, *History of the American Revolution,* 2:306–7; Paul C. Phillips, *The West in the Diplomacy of the American Revolution* (Urbana, Ill., 1913), p. 201; and Orville T. Murphy, "The Comte de Vergennes, the Newfoundland Fisheries, and the Peace Negotiation of 1783: A Reconsideration," *Canadian Historical Review* 46 (1965): 35.

depart from the "letter" or "spirit" of the alliance or "technically" violate the commitment in the alliance to conclude neither truce nor peace without first obtaining France's formal consent. They were not violators because the provisional treaty would not take effect until Britain and France had concluded their own preliminary treaty. At least this is the rationale of Benjamin Franklin, the wizard of diplomacy, and of the traditionalist scholars who dominate this aspect of alliance historiography.[41]

Yet some scholars challenge this involved rationale on behalf of an American innocence that may never have existed. They insist that the American commissioners were not at all victims of French guile and that these commissioners, not the French negotiators, violated treaty obligations. A few contemporaries of the peacemakers saw the diplomacy in Paris in the same light. James Madison, for one, thought that "the separate and secret manner in which our Ministers had proceeded with respect to France" departed from the sense of the alliance and was not justified by allegations of French deceit. Jared Sparks, an American historian, maintains that Jay's "suspicions have been assumed as historical facts." A modern scholar, John J. Meng, argues that "the term 'Provisional Articles' was nothing more than a legal fiction" and cannot justify American treaty violation. He insists that Adams and Jay were responsible for a "gross disregard of American treaty obligations to France."[42]

[41] See Corwin, *French Policy and Alliance*, p. 341; Bemis, *Diplomacy of the American Revolution*, pp. viii and 240; and Morris, *Peacemakers*, p. 385, who says dexterous Americans maintained "the semblance of the alliance."

[42] For the Madison quotation see Debates in the Congress . . . , Mar. 12–15, 1783, Gaillard Hunt, ed., *The Writings of James Madison*, 9 vols. (New York, 1900–1910), 1:404. See also Jared Sparks,

These dissenters hardly dented the conventional interpretation. It continues to be repeated in monographs and textbooks along with stories illustrating the innate shrewdness of the American innocents in Paris. For example, two weeks after the American commissioners had signed the preliminary terms with Britain, Vergennes angrily reprimanded them for circumventing the alliance in their secret diplomacy. Old Ben Franklin spoke up for his fellow commissioners, admitting that they had neglected the propriety one ally owed another. Foxily, however, he urged Vergennes not to make an issue of it. A clash at this point over treaty obligations would merely play into the hands of the British, who hoped to drive a wedge between France and the United States.

Vergennes accepted what the American diplomats had done because of Franklin's persuasiveness and because their action gave France an excuse to retreat from her embarrassing commitment to Spain to help recover Gibraltar. If freed from fighting in North America while the war continued elsewhere, Britain obviously would be a more formidable foe at Gibraltar. Vergennes did not wish to continue to struggle against a Britain still capable of inflicting considerable injury on French

"France and the United States during the American Revolution," in James B. Scott, ed., *The United States and France: Some Opinions on International Gratitude* (New York, 1926), p. 162; John J. Meng, "Franco-American Diplomacy and the Treaty of Paris, 1783," *Records of the American Catholic Historical Society of Philadelphia* 44 (1933): 216; Stinchcombe, *American Revolution and French Alliance,* p. 195; Stourzh, *Benjamin Franklin,* p. 173; and Felix Gilbert, "Bicentennial Reflections," *Foreign Affairs* 54 (1976): 639. A French writer, Faÿ, in his *Revolutionary Spirit in France and America,* p. 168, comments on "American duplicity." Jonathan R. Dull, "France and the American Revolution: Questioning the Myths," *Proceedings of the First Annual Meeting of the Western Society for French History* (Las Cruces, N.Mex., 1974), p. 116, attacks the "myth" of French betrayal.

forces. With his belated approval, therefore, the preliminary Anglo-American agreement, without substantive change, became the final treaty of peace signed in Paris on September 3, 1783. That treaty not only confirmed the independence of thirteen former colonies but also gave the United States an empire it had not conquered or occupied, the territory extending from the Appalachian Mountains to the Mississippi River.

In sum, American diplomats succeeded in clandestine negotiations because French leaders considered their European problems more pressing than any effort to force American adherence to the letter of the alliance. Thus, from the beginning of the new nation, according to a thesis that has among historians of foreign relations become virtually a cliché, Europe's distresses contributed to America's successes.

The story of the alliance does not end with the remarkable achievements of the American diplomats in Paris. Historians who continue the story usually also carry the theme of America profiting from Europe's distresses into the early national period. This theme does not arouse noteworthy controversy, but the value of the French alliance to the newly independent United States does. Was the alliance now an asset or a liability? A few writers, like Ben Franklin, contend that the safety of the new nation depended on remaining faithful to the alliance. Without it the United States would be at the mercy of a still powerful mother country. Franklin suggested that "it is our firm connexion with France, that gives us weight with England, and respect throughout Europe."[43]

Yet most historians of the Revolutionary era, from Edward Corwin to William C. Stinchcombe, conclude that the United States and France stopped acting as al-

[43] Benjamin Franklin to Samuel Cooper, Dec. 26, 1782, Jared Sparks, ed., *The Works of Benjamin Franklin*, 8th ed., 10 vols. (Boston, 1844), 9:463.

lies in 1782, when their national interests ceased to co-
incide. The alliance "faded away" in 1783, or it survived
in name only without vitality or effectiveness. Seeing no
further benefits to be derived from the pact, Americans
came to view it as an annoying entanglement or a both-
ersome anachronism. "The alliance was," according to
this general evaluation, "a temporary means to a noble
end" or "a marriage of convenience" rather than the
long-term commitment stated in its text.[44]

This kind of speculation is plausible because between
1783 and 1793 those who shaped policy in France had
to concentrate on political matters on the Continent or
on internal crises that brought revolution and foreign
wars. For Americans this was also a "critical period"
when they focused on boundary controversies, trade,
and pressing domestic issues, such as repairing an old
constitution or framing a new one. Neither French nor
American leaders seemed to have had much time to
ponder the status of their alliance.

Scholars who do not go along with the theory of early
termination demonstrate that even in the decade following Independence the alliance continued to hold an important, if not prominent, place in Franco-American
relations. It also occupied a controversial position in
American politics and foreign policy. It was, in the view
of Albert Hall Bowman, a historian of the Federalist
era, "the cornerstone of American foreign policy."[45]

[44] See Corwin, *French Policy and Alliance*, p. 358; Richard W. Van
Alstyne, *Genesis of American Nationalism* (Waltham, Mass., 1970), p.
108; Paul A. Varg, *Foreign Policies of the Founding Fathers* (East Lan-
sing, Mich., 1963), p. 25; Stinchcombe, *American Revolution and
French Alliance*, pp. 1, 3, 183, and 199–200; and Merrill Jensen, *The
New Nation: A History of the United States during the Confederation,
1781–1789* (New York, 1950), p. 6.

[45] *The Struggle for Neutrality: Franco-American Diplomacy during the
Federalist Era* (Knoxville, Tenn., 1974), p. 4. Noteworthy among others who, in varying degrees, see continuity in the history of the

When confronted with the theory that the alliance had died, French officials insisted that it remained in force. Vergennes, for instance, vigorously upheld continuity. "Those who have once been the allies of France," he asserted in reference to Americans, "are her allies always." Later, in 1788, when John Jay as secretary for foreign affairs also expressed doubt that the pact remained in effect, France's foreign minister, Armand-Marc, comte de Montmorin, countered that the king and his council were "singularly astonished" by this attitude. Montmorin suggested that Jay should reread the treaty's text; he would then note that it was perpetual. The king, the minister added, regarded the alliance as "inalterable."[46]

Those Americans who disliked this perpetual connection with France saw in occurrences flowing from the French Revolution of 1789 an opportunity to get rid of it. Events of 1792 and 1793, when revolutionaries abolished the monarchy, proclaimed France a republic, be-

alliance are: Alexander DeConde, *Entangling Alliance: Politics and Diplomacy under George Washington* (Durham, N.C., 1958); idem, *The Quasi-War: The Politics and Diplomacy of the Undeclared War with France, 1797–1801* (New York, 1966); Bradford Perkins, *The First Rapprochement: England and the United States, 1794–1805* (Philadelphia, 1955); Jerald A. Combs, *The Jay Treaty: Political Battleground of the Founding Fathers* (Berkeley, Calif., 1970); Peter P. Hill, *William Vans Murray, Federalist Diplomat: The Shaping of Peace with France, 1797–1801* (Syracuse, N.Y., 1971); and Kaplan, "Toward Isolationism: The Rise and Fall of the Franco-American Alliance, 1775–1801," pp. 134–60.

[46] Vergennes is quoted in George H. Guttridge, *David Hartley, M.P., an Advocate of Conciliation, 1774–1783* (Berkeley, Calif., 1926), p. 319, and Montmorin is quoted in Darling, *Our Rising Empire*, p. 117, but Darling adds, "Even so, both parties had abandoned their alliance for all practical purposes." John Adams earlier pointed out, as did Montmorin, not only that the alliance was perpetual, but that it could not "be satisfied and discharged" (Adams to Congress, Apr. 18, 1780, Adams, *Works of John Adams*, 7:149).

headed Louis XVI, and declared war against Britain, Holland, and Spain, brought the alliance to the forefront of American foreign policy. Since the two national political parties that were then in process of formation took opposing positions on the revolution in France, the alliance became a national political issue.

Secretary of the Treasury Alexander Hamilton, head of the Federalist party, considered the alliance to be dangerous because it could drag the United States into France's war against England. He urged the president to jettison the treaties of 1778, arguing that since the monarchy that had negotiated them had perished, they were no longer binding. In this instance George Washington did not follow Hamilton's advice. Instead, the president accepted essentially the view of Thomas Jefferson, then secretary of state and leader of the Republican party, that treaties bind nations not governments. The alliance therefore remained as much in effect with the French republic as it did with the monarchy.

The British, too, regarded the alliance as still in force and menacing as well. They reminded the American government that its commitment under the pact of 1778 was defensive and that since France had taken the initiative in declaring war, the United States was not bound by the alliance to intervene.[47]

Even though Federalists failed to sink the alliance, they were determined to block intervention under its terms in the war and to prevent its use for action favorable to France. On April 22, 1793, as urged by Hamilton, the president therefore issued a proclamation of neutrality advantageous to England.

At first this neutral stance did not disturb leaders of the French republic. They considered requesting Amer-

[47] See Charles R. Ritcheson, *Aftermath of Revolution: British Policy toward the United States, 1783–1795* (Dallas, Tex., 1969), pp. 273–74.

ican help under the alliance for defense of their West Indies if sorely needed and if Americans evinced an eagerness to fight. At this point, however, the French did not wish to draw Americans into the hostilities, mainly because they believed the United States could do little of consequence to affect the outcome of their European wars. Nonetheless, the French still considered the alliance a useful instrument of policy and expected to profit from it. They believed that as an ally the United States should act as a beneficent neutral, giving France special privileges and help, such as use of American ports for action against British commerce.

Edmond C. Genêt, French republicanism's first emissary to the United States, boldly sought such assistance on the basis of the alliance. He solicited collaboration in the arming of French privateers and in the recruiting of troops for invasion of Canada and Louisiana. Such help, apprehensive Federalists said, would provoke English retaliation. They demanded and obtained Genêt's recall.

Federalists also dreaded the possibility of an English attack on French islands in the Caribbean that could trigger a French request for American intervention under the alliance. When war with England seemed possible anyway over other issues, they averted it by sending John Jay on a special mission to London. The commercial treaty he negotiated in November 1794, along with the refusal of Washington's government to act as the faithful nonbelligerent ally that French leaders desired, provoked anger in Paris. French republicans viewed the English agreement as an alliance that violated America's obligations under their treaties of 1778. In the perspective of historian Paul A. Varg, "The Jay Treaty reduced the alliance to nullity."[48]

[48] The quotation comes from Varg, *Foreign Policies of the Founding Fathers,* p. 120. E. Wilson Lyon, "The Directory and the United

In retaliation the French violated their own obligations under the treaties of 1778, denounced the alliance, ruptured diplomatic relations, and attempted to manipulate politics in the United States. They hoped to drive the Federalists, whom they regarded as anti-alliance and pro-English, from power. They assumed that when Jeffersonian Republicans took over, whom they considered pro-French, the alliance would have the support it merited.

This French meddling and the political strife over foreign policy alarmed Washington, who considered opposition to his policies as faction. He decided not to seek a third term in the presidency and to leave the nation a valedictory against the French alliance. In his Farewell Address of September 19, 1796, he warned fellow Americans to have "as little political connection as possible" with Europe and "to steer clear of permanent alliances with any portion of the foreign world." Once an alliance, such as that with France, has served its purpose, he said, it breeds trouble. To many Americans, particularly to Federalists, Washington's advice seemed particularly appropriate in view of the difficulties with France.

This aspect of the conventional story uses the Farewell Address as the link between the alliance and the idea of an undesirable entanglement in European politics. Few scholars disagree with this connection, and most depict the address as an attack on the alliance.[49]

States," *American Historical Review* 43 (1938): 515, sees justification in the French view of Jay's treaty. See also Morison, *Harrison Gray Otis,* 1:59; and Georges Solovieff, "Franco-American Relations from 1775 to 1800," *American Society Legion of Honor Magazine* 48 (1977): 114.

[49] See Bowman, *Struggle for Neutrality,* p. 268; DeConde, *Entangling Alliance,* pp. 465–71; Kaplan, *Colonies to Nation,* pp. 256–57; Gilbert, *To the Farewell Address,* pp. 130–32; and Darling, *Our Rising Empire,* pp. 227–28.

When they attempt to explain Washington's motivation, however, assessments clash. Some writers argue that Washington saw peril to the nation from the alliance because it could drag Americans into a war which they did not want and which could not possibly benefit them. According to this interpretation by Samuel Flagg Bemis, Washington and Hamilton presented "an argument to open the door to an escape from the French alliance."[50] Others maintain that Washington's valedictory focuses on the danger to republican government arising from French interference in American domestic politics rather than on the alliance itself. Another thesis argues that Washington merely wished to rid the nation of an embarrassing connection to France because he and fellow Federalists desired a closer relationship, in effect an alliance, with England. Still another interpretation suggests that Washington and Hamilton designed the farewell as a political document to bring a Federalist victory in the presidential election of 1796. As Arthur Markowitz points out, they used the unpopular alliance as a scapegoat.[51]

This address and the experience with the alliance up to this point, as conveyed in conventional accounts, had a long-lasting influence on the nation. The concept of the French treaty as the inhibiting entanglement that Washington deplored inculcated in Americans an aversion to formal alliances that persisted until the United

[50] "Washington's Farewell Address: A Foreign Policy of Independence," *American Historical Review* 39 (1934): 267. See also DeConde, *Entangling Alliance,* p. 503.

[51] Arthur A. Markowitz, "Washington's Farewell and the Historians: A Critical Review," *Pennsylvania Magazine of History and Biography* 44 (1970): 173–91, analyzes various interpretations; *Washington's Farewell Address: The View from the Twentieth Century,* ed. Burton I. Kaufman (Chicago, 1969), offers analysis with selections from the literature on the subject.

States in April 1949 finally concluded another alliance with European nations, the North Atlantic Treaty. Scholars of various persuasions also claim that disillusionment with the alliance of 1778 stemming from that "classic statement of American isolationism," the Farewell Address, formed the backbone of an isolationism that persisted in American foreign policy well into the twentieth century.[52]

Washington's successor, John Adams, accepted the attitude toward the alliance expounded in the farewell. He also attempted to deal directly with the causes of the quarrel with France that he had inherited. He sent an extraordinary mission to Paris to resolve difficulties and "perhaps to abrogate or remodify the Treaty of Alliance."[53] When that effort, known as the XYZ affair, failed amidst revelations of French demands for bribes, the United States and France clashed in the Quasi War, an undeclared war fought mainly at sea. The Federalist establishment quickly placed the country on a war footing and enacted measures designed to gain public support for a full-scale conflict it desired.

In one of these laws passed on July 7, 1798, Congress unilaterally abrogated the treaties of 1778, using as justification France's previous violation of the agreements.

[52] The quotation comes from Kaufman, *Washington's Farewell*, p. 8. For pertinent speculation, see Gilbert, *To the Farewell Address*, p. 135; and Kaplan, "Toward Isolationism," p. 134. Williams, *Contours of American History*, pp. 173–74, dissents. He calls the address "a mercantilist manifesto for unchallengeable empire." For a slightly different analysis, see Williams, "The Age of Mercantilism: An Interpretation of the American Political Economy, 1763 to 1828," *William and Mary Quarterly*, 3d ser. 15 (1958): 426.

[53] Alexander Hamilton to Theodore Sedgwick, Feb. 26, 1797, Harold C. Syrett, ed., *The Papers of Alexander Hamilton*, 26 vols. to date (New York, 1961–), 20:522. See also Stephen G. Kurtz, *The Presidency of John Adams: The Collapse of Federalism, 1795–1800* (Philadelphia, 1957), pp. 284–85.

Federalists considered this a major achievement. "To be unfettered of the Treaty of alliance and its enslaving clauses of Guarantee," one of their officials commented, was one of the great benefits of the undeclared war. "I hope," he added, "we would then form no more Treaties of alliance with any Nation."[54]

Most historians of these events say the alliance died then, for a second time.[55] The French took a different attitude. Even though earlier France had on her own denounced the alliance, she refused to accept the American legislation as legally binding. Even during the heat of anger against American measures, France had not formally annulled the alliance. In October 1799 her foreign minister even fancifully expressed desire for a continuing close alliance with the United States at the end of hostilities.[56]

When peace negotiations began in the spring of 1800, Napoleon Bonaparte, a hardheaded realist, a soldier who had seized power in a coup, ruled France. He realized that the alliance was obsolete, but for bargaining purposes he refused to recognize the American annulment as valid and insisted that the pact still remained in force.[57] He could and did use the alliance as a bargaining chip because he knew Americans disliked it, con-

[54] James C. Mountflorence to Rufus King, Aug. 18, 1798, Rufus King Papers, Huntington Library, San Marino, Calif. Richard B. Morris, *The Emerging Nations and the American Revolution* (New York, 1970), p. 9, asserts that America fought the Quasi War to end the alliance.

[55] See, for example, Blumenthal, *France and the United States,* p. 15; and Marvin R. Zahniser, *Uncertain Friendship: American-French Relations through the Cold War* (New York, 1975), p. 76.

[56] Karl Friedrich Reinhard, discussed in Hill, *William Vans Murray,* p. 157.

[57] Most scholars consider Bonaparte correct in this view. See Darling, *Our Rising Empire,* pp. 376–78; and Bowman, *Struggle for Neutrality,* pp. 397 and 426–27n.

sidered it an albatross, and wished to be rid of it once and for all. When American peace commissioners agreed to economic concessions he desired, he accepted abrogation of the alliance in the Convention of Morfontaine, signed on September 30, 1800, that ended the Quasi War.

Eagerly sought in 1778, the French alliance received burial unlamented by either party. Technically, it lasted twenty-two years, almost a quarter of a century. Its effective life—five years—was much shorter, just long enough to help bring secure independence to the United States.

If there is in the rise and fall of the French alliance any consistency in behavior or principle among those who shaped it and destroyed it, I believed it lies in their conceptions of national self-interest. All these men— Americans, Frenchmen, and other Europeans—worked within a context of power politics whose rules they understood, accepted, and tried to bend. Self-interest is so broad and so flexible that men of power invariably stretch it to whatever shape appears necessary to serve their purposes. It also gives them leeway to twist rules, modify contracts, and reinterpret commitments.

Likewise, the ambiguity of self-interest permits historians to perceive the concept virtually as they see fit and, as in the instance of the alliance, to ramble in their speculations. Yet most scholars are aware that self-interest, or something akin to it, motivated the jealousies, suspicions, and devious maneuvers of all those involved in the larger diplomacy of the alliance, of Americans no less than of others. One of the earliest American interpreters of the alliance, David Ramsay, observed this kind of motivation, suggesting that "interest governs public bodies more than private persons."[58] Fortunately

---

[58] Ramsay, *History of the American Revolution*, 2:67. See also Blumenthal, *France and the United States*, p. 15.

for the United States when it needed the alliance most, the self-interest of France, as perceived by her elitist rulers, converged with its own. After Independence, from the perspective of the ruling establishment in the United States, divergence replaced convergence.

Much of the speculation on the history of the French alliance recognizes this shifting focus of self-interest within a pattern of power politics.[59] Power—how to attain it, hold it, and enhance it—is the essence of the game. When the conventional speculations take power and self-interest into account and are based on balanced scholarship, they usually remain solid and able to withstand revisionist assaults. When those speculations stem from ethnocentric predilections and nationalist bias, they are frequently flimsy, contradictory, or otherwise flawed and are prey to revisionist attacks. For example, when standard histories portray Americans within the story of the alliance as consistently virtuous and incorruptible and adversaries as sinister and deceitful, historians defy logic.

Despite such flaws, I must admit that like most academicians, and others too, I have been influenced in my own speculations on the French alliance by conventional interpretations. Not only do I view the alliance, as do traditionalists, as a key document in the nation's history, but I also still find the conventional story fascinating and sound in its essentials, and I still admire much of the scholarship that has passed it on for almost two hundred years. Even though I am critical of some aspects of the traditional verdicts, especially their ethnocentricity, I realize that historians, like the men who made and broke the alliance and who are usually re-

[59] For a recent appraisal on this theme, see Claude Fohlen, "The Impact of the American Revolution on France," in Library of Congress, *The Impact of the American Revolution Abroad* (Washington, D.C., 1976), p. 22.

vered as Founding Fathers, are fallible, prone to be influenced by nationalist emotions, and swayed by their
own perceived interests. For this reason, if for no other,
there most likely will always be reason to challenge conventional speculation on the history of the French alliance. It seems unlikely, however, that the challenges will
bring changes of substance to that speculation.

WILLIAM C. STINCHCOMBE

Americans Celebrate the Birth of the Dauphin

THE SIGNING OF the Franco-American alliance in February 1778 gave the newly formed republic of the
United States the vital support needed to win independence. Americans had been seeking an alliance with
France since 1776, when the Continental Congress secretly dispatched Silas Deane to France. Later that year
Congress appointed Benjamin Franklin and Arthur Lee
to join Deane as members of a commission to negotiate
a treaty with France. The proposed treaty was to follow
the concepts of the Model Treaty, written primarily by
John Adams and adopted by Congress in the late summer of 1776. The original purpose of the Declaration
of Independence was to form foreign alliances. But for
the first eighteen months of American independence
France remained noncommital. After the victory over
the British at Saratoga, however, the French indicated
their willingness to enter into a treaty. They insisted,
nevertheless, that a defensive alliance be negotiated in
addition to the commercial pact. Ignoring their instruc-

tions from Congress, the American commissioners accepted the French proposal and the two countries vowed to fight Great Britain until the independence of the United States was established. The treaty's binding article forbade either power to make a separate peace with Great Britain. When members of Congress learned of the two treaties in the first week of May 1778, they ratified them unanimously and without debate, thus entering into an alliance with his Most Christian Majesty, Louis XVI of France.

In retrospect the treaties with France seem to be an anomaly in United States foreign policy. The French alliance was to be the only political alliance entered into by the United States during its first 173 years of existence. The drive for independence desperately required a foreign alliance if it was to be successful. But many Revolutionary leaders also desired a quite different policy in foreign affairs. Thomas Paine's *Common Sense,* published in early 1776, and the Declaration of Independence six months later advanced the ideal of total separation not only from Great Britain but from all Europe. The New and Old worlds had long been considered distinct spheres, but the idea of separation did not become dominant until the era of the Revolution. Dissenters who had emigrated to America to rid themselves of state-controlled churches gave solid backing to the goal of American separation.

In the twenty-five years before the Revolution, economic changes also offered a basis for the separation argument. Trade with the West Indies grew rapidly during this period, as the sugar islands became an increasingly important market for the mainland colonies. American shipowners and merchants were gradually but perceptibly reducing the European foundation of their maritime prosperity. Although commerce with Great Britain continued to be important, especially for manufactured goods, farmers and planters exporting agricultural goods saw a decreasing need for political ties with Europe. Yet the French alliance took Americans and their independence movement into the maelstrom of European politics, making them more vulnerable to changes in the European balance of power than they had been under Great Britain's rule.

Certainly a hearty dose of realpolitik guided the actions of Revolutionary leaders in the conduct of foreign policy. Even so, the policy embarked upon in 1778 seemed to contradict many of the Revolution's internal goals. France was an absolutist state in which the toleration of Protestantism and other religions still received no official sanction by the government. Many colonists, moreover, held a stereotyped view of Frenchmen as devious and aggressive. Loyalists repeatedly noted the contradiction of a republic depending upon a Catholic monarchy for its freedom. Nevertheless, the press, clergy, and local elites did not openly protest the new foreign policy and for the most part worked diligently to make the alliance a success.[1] The transformation of politics that had occurred in the colonies during the struggle against Great Britain from 1763 to 1778 set the stage for the new foreign policy. Once independence became the Americans' primary goal, the ties with the mother country were not only cast aside but new departures could be made in foreign policy to assure the republic's survival.

Thus, the colonists reversed the position that they had taken in three wars fought during the previous seventy-five years between the English and the French. In these earlier wars the colonists had offered men and money to drive the hated French away from prospective

[1] William C. Stinchcombe, *The American Revolution and the French Alliance* (Syracuse, N.Y., 1969), pp. 91–117.

English settlements. While seeking territory, Americans also gave voice to a profound anti-Catholicism. American colonists were ecstatic in 1760, when the French were decisively defeated in Canada. After offering thanks to the guiding hand of Providence, many victory sermons asserted that American territorial aspirations must now be fulfilled.[2] The restrictive measures taken by the British government from 1763 through 1774 to prevent rapid American settlement, and the Quebec Act of 1774, seemed to many a betrayal of the victory. Americans responded by a dual hanging in effigy of the pope and George III. The pope was a traditional enemy ritually condemned on public occasions, but the addition of the king of England showed how the colonists could now include on their list of malefactors anybody who opposed American autonomy.

Although anti-Catholic sentiment was deep and pervasive in the colonies, it was not even a minor cause in the drive for American independence. In 1775, well before the Declaration of Independence, colonists launched another attack on Canada, for clearly strategic reasons. In what were futile measures Congress appealed to the Catholic peasantry to join the Revolution. Washington prohibited the celebration of Guy Fawkes Day by soldiers in Boston, because this event would hinder the effort to persuade Canadian Catholics to join the American cause. Thus long before the alliance Americans were willing to put aside the religious issue when it suited their purposes.

Accompanying Benjamin Franklin to Canada on a mission for Congress, for example, were the Catholics Charles Carroll of Carrollton and his cousin John Carroll, a priest. These Maryland Catholics worked with

[2] Samuel Woodward, *A Sermon Preached October 9, 1760* (Boston, 1760), pp. 11–16; John Mellen, *A Sermon Preached at the West Parish in Lancaster, October 9, 1760* (Boston, 1760), p. 36.

Franklin to bolster the image of the Revolution as a nonreligious war.[3] That the Canadian expedition failed and Canadian Catholics declined to join in large numbers does not qualify Americans' willingness to set aside religion when it interfered with politics.

Between 1778 and 1781, however, there were few demonstrations of public enthusiasm for the alliance except for the obligatory dinner in Philadelphia between the French ministers and members of Congress on the occasion of the king's birthday. But following the victory at Yorktown in October 1781 and the announcement of the birth of the dauphin in the summer of 1782, Americans held more celebrations in honor of their ally and the future heir to the throne than they had for any political event or cause since 1776. These festivities were prepared without direction from members of Congress, moreover. Without the victory at Yorktown, it is unlikely that France would have received this public acclaim. Nevertheless, the size and scope of the celebrations indicate the degree to which Americans had incorporated the foreign policy goals that Congress had adopted. The Revolution and its anticipated success were now becoming the basis for local and national politics.

An analysis of the fetes held after Yorktown and the birth of the dauphin will enable us to understand more about how local leaders accepted an alliance with a Catholic monarchy. Such an analysis will also reveal that Americans' future expectations were often at odds with the obligations of the French alliance. By studying the celebrations, we will have one indication of the extent to which the leadership of Congress was accepted after seven years of war.

[3] Gustave Lanctot, *Canada and the American Revolution, 1774–1783*, trans. Margaret M. Cameron (Cambridge, 1967), pp. 134–36.

Although Americans rejoiced in the alliance once victory was assured, few had thoroughly considered the ramifications of the pact with France. Americans rarely acknowledged, either publicly or privately, the presence of tension between the two countries on political issues. The celebrants did not define the United States in specific political terms pertaining to boundaries, commerce, or the fisheries. Because these conditions were only vaguely defined, the expectation of a certain victory allowed a flowering of religious and political freedom. The British had been defeated without granting France territory in North America.

The fortuitous circumstances leading to Yorktown have been described many times and need not be repeated, except to note the mounting tension caused by the French army's arrival in the United States. When Admiral d'Estaing moved to Boston in 1778 to refit, riots erupted between French and American sailors. Steps were quickly taken to suppress these incidents, but when French planners drew up General Rochambeau's instructions, they ordered him to keep his army isolated from Americans, particularly civilians, to prevent any needless exacerbation of tensions. Following his arrival in Newport in July 1780, Rochambeau ensconced himself there and then took no part in the summer campaign, much to Washington's chagrin.[4]

Rochambeau's forces did not leave Newport for eleven months, a period in which the American position rapidly deteriorated in the Carolinas and Virginia. A conservative in his approach to military tactics, Rochambeau refused American appeals that he divide his troops and send some into the southern theater. He had prom-

---

[4] Lee Kennett, *The French Forces in America, 1780–1783* (Westport, Conn., 1977), pp. 57 and 46.

ised on his arrival that he was leading only the advance force of a much larger French contingent, but Americans waited in vain for a second division to arrive.[5] The additional troops never left France, partly because of the British blockade of Brest but principally because the French government found it more economical to subsidize the American army than send their own men and ships.[6]

Deep-seated American prejudices about Frenchmen can be seen in the reactions to French troops at Newport. Americans widely believed Frenchmen to be lacking in virility, small in physique, or peculiar in odor. One French officer complained that the English—always the villains—had poisoned Americans' minds. "They had carried their insolence to the point of saying that we were dwarfs, pale, ugly, specimens who lived exclusively on frogs and snails."[7] Another noted, "The English have portrayed us to the Americans as pygmies."[8] That these images had currency can be seen in the comments of an American merchant who visited Newport. "Neither the Officers nor men are the effeminate Beings we were heretofore taught to believe

[5] Count de Rochambeau to Prince de Montbarey, July 16, 1780, Rochambeau Papers, VII, Library of Congress; *Newport Mercury,* Aug. 12, 1780.

[6] "Rapport au Roi sur l'augmentation de troupes et munitions demande par Rochambeau," Mar. 8, 1781, Archives du Ministère des Affaires Etrangères, Correspondance Politique (hereafter cited as AAE, CP), Etats-Unis, 20; Memoire dur l'Amerique, n.d., ibid., 21.

[7] Oct. 1780, the comte de Clermont-Crèvecoeur, "Journal of the War in America during the Years 1780, 1781, 1782, 1783," ed. and trans. Howard C. Rice, Jr., and Anne S. K. Brown, *The American Campaigns of Rochambeau's Army, 1780, 1781, 1782, 1783,* 2 vols. (Princeton and Providence, 1972), 1:21.

[8] Kennett, *French Forces in America,* p. 135.

them," he explained; "they are as large & as likely men as can be produced by any nation."[9]

Although the behavior of the French troops at Newport was exemplary and the conduct of the officers correct, Americans grew pessimistic following defeats in the South, mutinies in the American army in 1780–81, and increasing dependence on French financial, naval, and military aid. The loyalist press accurately reported that the Americans "were surprised at the Inactivity of their Allies the French, who they say have done nothing since their arrival in America but eat Provisions designed for the Army under the Command of General Washington."[10] In another effort to arouse the anticipated animosity between the French and Americans, a loyalist asserted, "A good Frenchman loves Monarchy and let matters go how they may, will never permit a Republic to be established on the American continent," a thought that some Americans echoed privately.[11]

The early summer of 1781 marked the nadir of American military and diplomatic fortunes. This circumstance accounted for the exaggerated praise that Americans gave the French army as it finally left Newport and marched south. Many papers reported that "the exact discipline of the troops, and the attention of the officers to prevent any injury to individuals have made the march of this army through the country very agreeable to the inhabitants." Showing more faith than accuracy, the writer emphasized that "not a single dis-

[9] William Channing to Ezra Stiles, Aug. 6, 1780, Franklin B. Dexter, ed., *The Literary Diary of Ezra Stiles,* 3 vols. (New York, 1901), 2:458–59.

[10] *New York Gazette,* Oct. 23, 1780.

[11] *Royal Gazette* (New York), Aug. 25, 1781; Thomas Tilliston to Robert R. Livingston, Robert R. Livingston Papers, Box 7, New-York Historical Society.

agreeable circumstance has taken place."[12] What local leaders and editors had tacitly decided was that incidents between the army and the inhabitants were not fit to print. A murder of an American civilian was reported only in the loyalist press. A waterfront brawl between Frenchmen and Americans in Boston, resulting in one death and numerous injuries, went unreported. Pillage and plundering by the French troops around New York City were also ignored.[13] Distrust of the French was never dissipated, and only by concentrating on the British and loyalists did American leaders and editors gloss over the troubles caused by a foreign army on American soil.

When the army arrived in Philadelphia on its march to Yorktown in early September 1781, it paraded before Congress and the citizenry: "the appearance of these troops far exceeds any thing of the kind seen on this continent, and presages the happiest success to the cause of America." One editor, Francis Bailey, assured his readers that the French soldiers were in good health and demonstrated the "utmost ardor to face the common enemy wherever he may lurk." Just as the army left Philadelphia, news arrived that Admiral de Grasse had defeated a British attempt to bring relief to Yorktown and that the junction of his ships with those from Newport under Admiral de Barras had occurred.[14] The trap had been sprung, and American hopes were high in the weeks before the final announcement of victory.

[12] *Freeman's Journal* (Philadelphia), Sept. 5, 1781; *Pennsylvania Packet* (Philadelphia), Sept. 6, 29, 1781; *Maryland Gazette* (Annapolis), Sept. 20, 1781; *New Jersey Gazette* (Trenton), Oct. 3, 1781; *Providence Gazette*, Oct. 6, 1781.

[13] Kennett, *French Forces in America*, pp. 80–87, 120, and 137.

[14] *Freeman's Journal*, Sept. 5, 1781.

Just before the official news of the expected victory at Yorktown, "A Republican" summarized the events of the previous six months in a widely reprinted essay. He reviewed the lack of troops, money, credit, and commerce that had afflicted the United States. Now, however, the prospects were truly glorious. The performances of the French army and fleet "claim the best returns of preference and gratitude of every American," from those "whose eyes are not meanly shut by the policy of early inculcated prejudices." He reminded his readers, however, that the "real cause of union lies not so much in principles of generosity as in reciprocal interest" between the two nations. Nevertheless, in Louis XVI's action the writer saw "a passion for doing good . . . void of calculations of policy." The essay concluded on a note that indicated the new opinion held of the French before the victory. "The allied army under the auspices of our great commander in chief, in Virginia, exhibits a prospect full of the most favourable impressions, and auguring the happiest issue to America."[15]

The story of the Yorktown battle, by which the alliance was crowned with laurels of success, is well known. Yet according to a recent interpretation, the low point in relations between the French and American armies came immediately after Yorktown.[16] Why this was so is not clear, but part of the answer may be that the French were shocked at the retaliation practiced by Americans after victory. For the French, it had not been their war; nor was it their kind of war. But Americans, whose future positions depended on victory, felt the frustrations of many years' struggle. These feelings found

[15] *Maryland Gazette,* Oct. 25, 1781; the letter is dated from Cambridge, Oct. 15, 1781.

[16] Kennett, *French Forces in America,* p. 156.

expression in a systematic policy of revenge against British officers and, particularly, against loyalists, who most threatened Americans' conception of themselves. From George Washington and Nathanael Greene on down to the militia leaders, brutal punishment of the enemy had become an accepted practice of warfare. To be gracious in victory had become impossible. One French officer commented on the difference between the European professional armies and the Americans, who desired to annihilate their enemies: "The English and the French got on famously with one another. When the Americans expressed their displeasure on this subject, we replied that good upbringing and courtesy bind men together, and that, since we had reason to believe that the Americans did not like us, they should not be surprised at our preferences [for the English]. Actually you never saw a French officer with an American. Although we were on good enough terms, we did not live together. This was, I believe, most fortunate for us. Their character being so different from ours, we should inevitably have quarreled."[17]

The news of Cornwallis's capitulation first spread through the United States by a letter from Admiral de Grasse to Governor Lee of Maryland. The *Pennsylvania Evening Post* printed the news three days after the victory, reminding the citizens of Philadelphia that "orders will be issued for preserving decorum becoming this glorious occasion."[18] The official celebration was held on October 24, following the arrival of Tench Tilghman, who carried Washington's official account. Instructions were issued to the inhabitants to light their candles at six and leave them on until nine. The

[17] Oct. 29, 1781, Clermont-Crèvecoeur, "Journal," *American Campaigns of Rochambeau*, 1:64.

[18] *Pennsylvania Evening Post* (Philadelphia), Oct. 22, 1781.

broadside noted that "decorum and harmony are earnestly recommended to every Citizen, and a general discountenance to the least appearance of riot."[19]

Such moral strictures underlay the growing fear of loss of control by many American leaders. Robert Morris commented that members of Congress did not find the celebration a completely joyful occasion, reminding his compatriots of the "distresses our Country has been exposed to, the Calamities we have repeatedly suffered, the perilous situation which our affairs have always been in." Not unexpectedly, riots broke out in Philadelphia, where those who had been lukewarm to the policies of Congress found their houses attacked. These Philadelphians were loyalist-inclined or, more often, just Quakers. Elizabeth Drinker wrote that the riot continued for three hours, leaving her house with seventy panes of glass broken and two doors ruined by stones and other objects. Her husband's shop was looted extensively. Anna Rawle, a loyalist and a Quaker, described the riot in her diary. The mob "broke the shutters and glass of the windows." The victory celebrants were about to break into the house until friends effected a timely rescue and prudently lit some candles. After submitting to the crowd's demands, she heard for two hours "the disagreeable noise of stones banging about, glass crashing, and tumultuous voices in the neighbourhood."[20] The good whig Jacob Hiltzheimer noted that he was "sorry to have to add, that many doors and windows were destroyed by a set of people who have no

[19] Broadside, Philadelphia, Oct. 24, 1781.

[20] Robert Morris, Diary, Nov. 3, 1781, E. James Ferguson, ed., *The Papers of Robert Morris, 1781–1784,* 4 vols. to date (Pittsburgh, 1973–), 3:131; "A Loyalist's Account of Certain Occurrences in Philadelphia after Cornwallis's Surrender at Yorktown," *Pennsylvania Magazine of History and Biography* 16 (1892): 104–7.

name."[21] The members of the crowd were not so anonymous or unknown as Hiltzheimer implied, however. Rather, the patriots' moral authority had been weakened by the rigors of war and their enemies ostracized. When victory came, these opponents found themselves sacrificed to the mob in the name of liberty and independence.

The editor of the *New Jersey Gazette*, Isaac Collins, assured his readers that the celebration in Trenton was "conducted with the greatest good order and propriety; and we mention it with pleasure, that not the least disturbance or irregularity happened during the whole festivity."[22] Of course if any vandalism occurred in Trenton, it is unlikely that it would have been mentioned. Newspapers reported no disturbances, despite repeated private accounts of pillage. In Salem, Mass., the news of Yorktown was treated with a gravity befitting that community, and it was reported that "the greatest joy and satisfaction were shown, in this and neighbouring towns, on the receipt of this most interesting intelligence."[23]

Other celebrations took similar forms. Rarely were overt political statements made in the aftermath of victory. In Newburgh, however, an army garrison burned Benedict Arnold in effigy for his treason. Much more typical was the experience of Providence, where a ship carrying handbills arrived October 27, after which an unidentified "Gentleman of Virginia" put on a "splendid Ball" with an exhibition of fireworks.[24] At Prince-

[21] Oct. 24, 1781, "Extracts from the Diary of Jacob Hiltzheimer of Philadelphia, 1768–1798," *Pennsylvania Magazine of History and Biography* 16 (1892): 160.

[22] *New Jersey Gazette*, Oct. 31, 1781.

[23] *Salem Gazette* (Mass.), Nov. 1, 1781.

[24] *Connecticut Courant* (Hartford), Nov. 6, 1781; *Providence Gazette*, Oct. 27, 1781.

ton, of all places, celebrants gathered at noon at a local tavern, where, we are told, they imbibed wine and punch. This celebration continued six hours, the readers being assured that the "company broke decently." We have no further information as to whether customary decorum was maintained.[25]

The toasts at victory parties indicate the order of appreciation that many unidentified citizens accorded to the leaders and events of the day. Almost inevitably thirteen toasts were offered, except in Trenton, where they forgot to salute Governor Livingston and added a fourteenth. Among political institutions Congress received first honor; the king of France was next acknowledged. Very little political comment appeared in the toasts, however, except for the routine appeal for peace with honor. At Princeton one toast honored "the friends of liberty everywhere," a statement that became a standard refrain in the coming months.[26]

In the victory celebrations Washington received foremost honor, followed most often by de Grasse, then Greene, who had led the successful southern army in the Carolinas, and then Rochambeau. In a strict ordering of recognition the contributions of the French troops received notice only after those of de Grasse and the Americans. This reflected a tendency to downplay the amount of French participation in the victory.[27] A letter from an "Officer in the Allied Army" reveals the same ordering. After praise for "our illustrious Commander," he thought that the "well concerted and ani-

[25] *New Jersey Gazette*, Oct. 31, 1781.

[26] Ibid.

[27] *Pennsylvania Packet*, Nov. 1, 1781; *Continental Journal* (Boston), Nov. 22, 1781; *New Jersey Gazette*, Oct. 31, 1781; *Salem Gazette*, Nov. 15, 1781; *Freeman's Journal*, Nov. 14, 1781; *Independent Chronicle* (Boston), Nov. 14, 21, 1781.

mated support of Count de Grasse . . . deserves the grateful plaudit of every American." The officer went on to extol Rochambeau's efforts and those of his army, concluding that their actions "can never be excelled, and only equaled by their American friends, who glowed with the laudable ambition of imitating the achievement of the finest body of men in the world."[28]

To mark the victory, members of Congress marched off to church en masse not once but twice, after having first given official thanks to all parties. Congressional chaplain Duffield conducted the first service in his Lutheran church. The second took place in a Catholic, or "Romish," as Robert Morris called it, church, the sermon given by Abbé de Bandole, a priest attached to the French legation in Philadelphia.[29] The attendance of members of Congress at a Catholic service was commented upon privately but attacked openly only in the loyalist press, in which it was alleged that Americans had now become Frenchmen and even advocated a repudiation of Congress.[30] One writer extended his denunciation to the point of assuring readers that Washington was in the service of Louis XVI and "that every American soldier of this alliance is now become in every sense a *Frenchman*." Congress, he asserted, now had influence only through "the Frenchified Mr. Washington alone."[31]

[28] *Connecticut Courant,* Nov. 13, 1781.

[29] *New Jersey Gazette,* Dec. 5, 1781; *Freeman's Journal,* Nov. 21, 1781; *Pennsylvania Packet,* Nov. 27, 1781; Connecticut Delegates to Jonathan Trumbull, Oct. 25, 1781, Edmund C. Burnett, ed., *Letters of Members of the Continental Congress,* 8 vols. (Washington, D.C., 1921–36), 6:250–51; Morris Diary, Nov. 3, 1781, Ferguson, *Papers of Robert Morris,* 3:131.

[30] *Royal Gazette,* Dec. 6, 1781.

[31] Ibid., Nov. 7, 1781.

The charges contained at least a kernel of truth. American soldiers were paid with French money on their way to Yorktown, transported by French ships, outnumbered by French soldiers and marines in battle, and protected by a French fleet at a site chosen by French political and military leaders. One response to loyalists' charges revealed more bravado than logic on a sensitive issue: "Formerly the fraternity at New York reproached us for paying our army with paper rags. They now fret and are displeased that we pay them with a loan from France, which they rationally suppose will metamorphose our army into Frenchmen and catholics. Surely we ought to thank these gentlemen for their benevolence, brotherly care, and officious concern for the welfare and morals of the American Army. Many People, however, are of the opinion, that it would become them better to provide for the safety of the remnant of their own." [32]

American editors took special pains to drive home the victory to their arch-tormentors, the loyalists in New York. Shortly after Yorktown a long advertisement supposedly from Rivington's paper appeared, presenting a new list of books and maps for sale. Loyalists could buy *The History of the American war: or the glorious exploits of Generals Gage, Howe, Burgoyne, Cornwallis and Clinton* or *A Full and true account of the conquest of the four Southern rebel colonies: with notes critical and explanatory by Lord Cornwallis.* Under maps appeared "an elegant map for the British Empire in America upon a *Very Small* scale." [33] Satire became reality in 1783 when loyalist editor Hugh Gaine advertised six months before the British departure a new map of the United States of

[32] *Connecticut Courant*, Dec. 4, 1781.

[33] *Norwich Packet* (Conn.), Dec. 6, 1781; *New Jersey Gazette*, Nov. 28, 1781.

America with "an allegorical Print of the Independence of America, and the Portraits of Gen. Washington, Dr. Franklin, and Mr. Laurens."[34]

In these continuing skirmishes, American editors offered little comment on Abbé de Bandole's sermon to Congress, which incorporated Enlightenment ideas to a greater extent than did the sermons of many American ministers discussing Yorktown. In the text, as reprinted in the rebel press, he told members of Congress that their cause had its first support in justice alone. He then continued, in a passage indistinguishable from Americans' own views of themselves, "You present to the universe the noble fight of a society, which is founded in equality and justice." The American government had secured to individuals "the utmost happiness which can be derived from human institutions." And, he noted, "this advantage, which so many other nations have been unable to procure, even after ages of effort and misery, is granted by divine providence to the United States."[35]

While Bandole had extolled French-American cooperation, Timothy Dwight mentioned France only once in his thirty-four-page sermon on the victory at Yorktown. In his single reference he observed that France, as well as Spain, had challenged English sea power, but he said nothing about French contributions to Yorktown.[36] For Dwight the evil nature of the English offered a sufficient topic, and he did not use the

[34] *New York Gazette & Weekly Mercury,* June 23, 1783.

[35] *Freeman's Journal,* Nov. 21, 1781.

[36] Timothy Dwight, *A Sermon Preached at Northhampton on the twenty-eighth of November, 1781* (Hartford, 1781), pp. 23–24; others mentioned the French role more frequently than did Dwight; see, for example, James Madison, *A Sermon Preached in the County of Botetourt on the 13th of December, 1781* (Richmond, 1781); Nathan Fiske, *An Oration delivered at Brookfield, Nov. 14, 1781* (Boston, 1781).

Yorktown victory as a means of discussing religious toleration, as other ministers did.[37]

The duc de Lauzun carried the news of the Yorktown victory back to Versailles, but his announcement was overshadowed by the birth of a dauphin, thus ending years of speculation and apprehension in France. The birth was first announced in the United States at Williamsburg, where much of the French army was stationed for the winter.[38] Three months later the Providence newspaper announced the birth, and it seemed at first that the event would pass without extensive comment in the United States.[39] But as the victory at Yorktown strengthened the resolve of the United States and France to seek a punitive peace treaty with Great Britain, based on their combined success, it seemed a propitious occasion to reaffirm American loyalty to the alliance.

The origins of the celebrations for the dauphin's birth were totally political, which is not surprising. Anne César, chevalier de La Luzerne, the French minister to the United States, carefully studied the political needs of the alliance and attempted to arrange events accordingly. Nevertheless, the size and purpose of the parties for the dauphin have gone relatively unnoticed. One scholar, Gillian Anderson, has uncovered a number of songs and poems written in the dauphin's honor.[40] Sym-

[37] Stinchcombe, *American Revolution and French Alliance,* pp. 98–103.

[38] Jan. 10–15, 1782, Evelyn Acomb, ed., *The Revolutionary Journal of Baron Ludwig Von Closen, 1780–1783* (Chapel Hill, N.C., 1958), pp. 171–72.

[39] *Providence Gazette,* Mar. 9, 1782.

[40] My thanks to Gillian Anderson, who provided me with the following list of newspapers carrying songs printed for the birth of the dauphin: *Newport Mercury,* Aug. 30, 1782; *Independent Gazetteer* (Phil-

bolically, the celebrations of the birth offered Americans a chance to bid farewell to the French, to recognize the value of their aid and alliance. This remained implicit in the celebrations, at least thirty to forty of which were held throughout the summer of 1782. In newspaper coverage at least eighty, and probably closer to one hundred, articles appeared in American papers describing the celebrations.[41] No other event during the Revolution, with the possible exception of the Silas Deane affair, received so much concentrated attention in the American press.

The widespread nature of the celebrations can be accounted for in part because of the changed political and military conditions arising from Yorktown. In the early months of 1782 Lord North desperately tried to retain power. After a series of defeats, however, the North cabinet resigned, to be replaced by an unstable coalition headed by Lord Rockingham. Parliament had decreed in strong terms that no offensive warfare was to take place in the United States. Charles James Fox, a consistent critic of the American war, assumed office as foreign secretary and Lord Shelburne, as colonial secretary. All of the news recounting these transformations in British policy had reached the United States by

adelphia), June 20, July 20, 1782; *Boston Evening Post,* June 28, Aug. 24, 1782; *Boston Gazette,* July 1, 1782; *New York Packet* (Fishkill), June 13, 1782; *New Jersey Journal* (Chatham), June 5, 1782; *The Massachusetts Spy* (Worcester), June 27, 1782.

[41] Because of duplications, the exact number is not easily determined except with qualifications. Newspapers covered for this statement include the following: *Salem Gazette, Boston Evening Post, Continental Journal, Independent Chronicle, Boston Gazette, Connecticut Courant, Norwich Packet, Newport Mercury, Providence Gazette, Royal Gazette, New York Gazette, New Jersey Gazette, Pennsylvania Packet, Freeman's Journal, Pennsylvania Journal* (Philadelphia), *Pennsylvania Gazette* (Philadelphia), *Independent Gazetteer, Virginia Gazette* (Richmond), and *Maryland Gazette.*

the time La Luzerne made his official announcement of the birth of the dauphin.[42]

Charles James Fox wanted to adopt a policy of opening negotiations on the basis of granting the United States independence. He then planned to concentrate British efforts on limiting the victory of France and Spain. But he lacked total control of the peace negotiations because Lord Shelburne, the king's personal choice, pursued the old policy of trying to divide the Continental Congress by sending special instructions to General Guy Carleton and Admiral Robert Digby. Shelburne's ill-fated efforts resembled Lord North's proposals to negotiate with Congress through the Howe brothers in 1776–77 and the Carlisle Commission in 1778. Carleton, who succeeded Henry Clinton as commander of the British forces in America, and Digby were directed first to try to open negotiations with Congress, and if that procedure failed, then to negotiate with the separate states. In addition to this approach, Shelburne sent representatives to Paris to commence negotiations with Franklin. Not until July, however, when Rockingham died and Shelburne assumed the role of head of the cabinet, thus causing Fox's resignation, did Shelburne direct all of the British peace negotiations.

Thus, underlying the celebrations for the dauphin was knowledge of the first serious efforts to negotiate a peace settlement based on independence. George III had been forced to acknowledge that his previous policy had become untenable. Furthermore, the French foreign minister, the comte de Vergennes, made it clear in

[42] On the peace negotiations in Europe, see Richard B. Morris, *The Peacemakers: The Great Powers and American Independence* (New York, 1965), pp. 248–310; Jonathan R. Dull, *The French Navy and American Independence: A Study of Arms and Diplomacy, 1774–1787* (Princeton, 1975), pp. 262–335.

the preliminary talks with British representatives that the peace parley must be conducted on the premise of American independence. When Americans rejoiced in 1782, peace with independence was assumed, if not assured. The French alliance had helped secure the major aim of American policy, and the outpouring of sympathy can be attributed in large part to this.

In April 1782 Vergennes ordered La Luzerne to see that Congress did not open negotiations with the British in the United States.[43] If at all possible, Vergennes wanted Congress to reaffirm its previous positions that all peace negotiations would take place in Europe, under French guidance. The news of the changes in British policy reached the United States in the first week of May 1782.[44] Members of Congress and other Americans realized that peace negotiations had probably started in Paris, although Congress went without official word from United States ministers for almost six months in 1782.

La Luzerne reported that Americans showed no inclination to negotiate with Shelburne's representatives, General Carleton and Admiral Digby, a point that he reaffirmed in the summer and fall of 1782.[45] To underscore French desires and reenforce commitment to the alliance, La Luzerne decided to announce the birth of the dauphin officially to Congress and did so in the second week of May. This, he informed Vergennes, would serve to bolster support for peace negotiations in Europe. He added that he had indicated his desire that

[43] The comte de Vergennes to the chevalier de La Luzerne, Apr. 9, 1782, AAE, CP, Etats-Unis, 21.

[44] *New York Gazette,* May 6, 1782; *Royal Gazette,* May 8, 1782; *Pennsylvania Packet,* May 2, 1782; *Pennsylvania Journal,* May 4, 1782.

[45] La Luzerne to Vergennes, May 6, 18, 29, June 3, 14, July 22, 28, Aug. 12, Sept. 28, 1782, AAE, CP, Etats-Unis, 21, 22.

Congress and the states confirm their loyalty to the alliance. Although he was not a humble man, La Luzerne found himself genuinely surprised at the outpouring in response to his suggestion. His claims that Americans displayed universal joy over the dauphin's birth and that the celebrations were "in no way my work" should not be taken too seriously, however.[46]

La Luzerne's announcement to Congress was treated with the grave dignity befitting a state occasion. The only sour note seems to have come from Robert R. Livingston, the foreign secretary, who complained because he was not invited to the party given by Congress after the announcement.[47] The Rhode Island delegates wrote that the "joy of Congress on this happy occasion will be manifested by a discharge of cannon, a display of fireworks, and by an elegant entertainment for the Minister of France."[48] James Madison, who wrote the reply to La Luzerne for the president of Congress, indicated a more realistic understanding of the purposes of the affair. "It was deemed politic," he wrote, "at this crisis to display every proper evidence of affectionate attachment to our Ally."[49]

La Luzerne decided to reciprocate and arranged a grand gala for Congress in mid-July. He chose this date

[46] La Luzerne to Vergennes, May 14, 1782, ibid., 21.

[47] Robert R. Livingston to John Hanson, May 8, 1782; Charles Thompson to Livingston, May 9, 10, 1782, Burnett, *Letters of Continental Congress*, 6:346–47.

[48] Rhode Island Delegates to William Greene, May 7, 1782, ibid., pp. 343–44.

[49] Report on Form of Public Audience for La Luzerne, May 7–9, 1782; Revised Reply of President of Congress to La Luzerne, May 8–12, 1782; James Madison to Edmund Randolph, May 14, 1782, William C. Hutchinson et al., eds., *The Papers of James Madison*, 12 vols. to date (Chicago and Charlottesville, Va., 1962–), 4:211, 222, and 242.

because Washington and Rochambeau had come to Philadelphia to confer on a strategy by which the French forces would undertake no more battles on the North American continent. The French agreed only to pass by New York in an effort to delay the departure of British troops for the West Indies. La Luzerne planned to announce that no more French military aid was forthcoming and at the same time to celebrate the alliance.[50]

The lavishness of La Luzerne's celebration amazed even Philadelphians, who were rapidly growing accustomed to luxury.[51] Utilizing a design by Pierre L'Enfant, who took leave of the American army to offer his services, La Luzerne added two pavilions to John Dickinson's rented town house for this occasion.[52] One pavilion was for dancing, the orchestra provided by the French army, with special boxes arranged for honored participants. Showing his usual care not to offend any group's sensibilities, La Luzerne ordered curtains on the boxes where Quakers were seated. He arranged the creation of an artificial garden with "hundreds of glass lamps" and a dining area to seat four hundred for a meal. This meal began at one in the morning and was described as "a cold-collation, simple, frugal, and elegant, and handsomely set off with a dessert consisting of cakes and all the fruits of the season."[53] To prepare

[50] La Luzerne to Vergennes, July 3, 15, 1782, AAE, CP, Etats-Unis, 21.

[51] Whitfield Bell, Jr., "Some Aspects of the Social History of Pennsylvania, 1760–1790," *Pennsylvania Magazine of History and Biography* 62 (1938): 297 and 300.

[52] *Freeman's Journal*, July 31, Aug. 30, 1782; Acomb, *Journal of Von Closen*, pp. 229–30; Benjamin Rush to Elizabeth Ferguson, July 16, 1782, Lyman Butterfield, ed., *Letters of Benjamin Rush*, 2 vols. (Princeton, 1951), 1:278–84.

[53] Ibid., p. 281.

the food, La Luzerne borrowed thirty cooks from the French army as well as a detachment of soldiers to protect the garden from intruders.

A French officer passing through Philadelphia in September described some of the decorations on the walls:

> At the east end of the room was a rising sun surmounted by 13 stars (and the arms of America) with an Indian watching the sunrise and apparently dazzled by its rays. Beside the Indian in the same picture was a woman, representing England, emptying a sack of gold into the hands of another Indian, who throws the gold at her feet with obvious contempt. At the opposite end of the room were the arms of France with a sun at its zenith lighting the world. And there were several other emblems appropriate to the event that had occasioned the fete. The pavilion was 100 feet long; its walls were supported by a colonnade of 30 to 40 feet high.[54]

In addition to the fifteen hundred invited guests, an additional crowd estimated to be in the thousands gathered outside. At first La Luzerne planned to distribute wine and gold coins to the assemblage, but he was dissuaded by fears of a riot, so a massive fireworks display was substituted instead. The Pennsylvania militia controlled street traffic for blocks around. Afterwards La Luzerne submitted a special bill to the foreign office for over five thousand dollars, not including French army expenses.[55]

Benjamin Rush left a detailed description of this

[54] Sept. 1782, Clermont-Crèvecoeur, "Journal," *American Campaigns of Rochambeau*, 1:77.

[55] La Luzerne to Vergennes, July 25, 1782, AAE, CP, Etats-Unis, 21.

party to celebrate the alliance. He was too much of an ideologue not to see the irony of the situation: "How great the revolution in the mind of an American! to rejoice in the birth of a prince whose religion he has been taught to consider unfriendly to humanity. And above all, how new the phenomenon for republicans and freemen to rejoice in the birth of a prince who must one day be the support of a monarchy and slavery: There are no prejudices so strong, no opinions so sacred, and no contradictions so palpable, that will not yield to the love of liberty." Rush could not avoid a few tart comments on his many enemies, however. He wrote that "the celebrated author of *Common Sense* retired frequently from company to analyze his thoughts and to enjoy the repast of his own original ideas." Surveying the crowd, Rush noted the presence of "the learned faculty of the college, and with them many who knew not whether Cicero plead in Latin or Greek, or whether Horace was a Roman or a Scotchman." He noted among the guests "whigs and men who formerly bore the character of tories."[56]

In the occasion that Rush described as a major social event of Philadelphia not only La Luzerne but some Americans began to leave the divisions of the war behind them. For former tories and Quakers to find themselves invited to the same event as members of Congress, French generals, and American military leaders indicates the assurance of victory felt by one group and the acknowledgment of a new order by the other group. This celebration and others throughout the United States marked the assumption of power by a new elite, in control following the victory over Great Britain.

The lavishness and indulgence of the parties did not

[56] Rush to Ferguson, July 16, 1782, Butterfield, *Letters of Rush,* 1:279 and 280.

go unnoticed by others. Republican simplicity was a slogan, not a reality. As John Beatty stood in the crowd outside at La Luzerne's gala, he noted changes that had taken place in Philadelphia since his last visit there two years before. "I am bold to say," he wrote his brother, "that this city will vie with the first Courts of Europe in dissipation, luxury, and extravagance, and sorry I am so young a Country should have so ill a precedent set them." He complained that special silks had been purchased by women and even many men wore silk with embroidery, concluding with the comment that "we poor *Mohair Gentry* were obliged to stand aloof."[57]

In the months following La Luzerne's announcement, organizations in different cities attempted to demonstrate their elation at the dauphin's birth. When the official congratulations of three states, Virginia, Rhode Island, and North Carolina, were delayed, the respective governors felt compelled to explain that this was only accidental and not because of any hesitancy about rejoicing over the dauphin.[58] In conducting this civic feast, Americans resorted freely to hyperbole. It was suggested that "in universally agreeing to shew their friendship for and gratitude to the French nation" at the birth of the dauphin, Americans were also wishing him a long life so that he might become like his father and "be a friend and guardian of the rights of mankind."[59]

---

[57] John Beatty to Reading and Erkuries Beatty, July 16, 1782, Joseph M. Beatty, ed., "Letters of the Four Beatty Brothers of the Continental Army, 1774–1794," *Pennsylvania Magazine of History and Biography* 44 (1920): 228–29.

[58] Edmund Randolph to James Madison, July 18, 1782, Hutchinson, *Papers of Madison,* 4:423; *Providence Gazette,* Aug. 17, 1782; *Pennsylvania Packet,* Aug. 17, 1782.

[59] *Freeman's Journal,* July 31, 1782.

A widely reprinted interpretation of the parties for the dauphin was written by Samuel Cooper of Boston. A Francophile, Cooper had served for years as a paid propagandist of the French government. Perhaps because of his experience of working for a monarchy while advocating a republic, Cooper could use this occasion to advance both French and American interests. In his summary Cooper noted in his usual paternal style that "every order of men in its own way, shouted benediction to the Dauphin." This was a compliment to the people's patriotism and also demonstrated the "good sense of the people who realized the importance in an hereditary Kingdom of such an event." The dauphin would be educated for the throne and may "save immense bloodshed which so often happens where the right of the crown is disputed." Cooper concluded that this was the "reason why even republicans, as far as they are friends of mankind, may rejoice when the heir to a great empire is born."[60]

Class distinctions abound in references made at the celebrations. The republic was clearly thought to incorporate deference to the newly acknowledged leaders. The apotheosis of Washington as the hero of the Revolution had already started.[61] Civilian leaders such as John Hancock, Sam and John Adams, John Jay, Robert Morris, Thomas Jefferson, and Benjamin Franklin, among others, went unmentioned in the toasts except for the obligatory salute to the local governor. No

[60] The same story appeared in the *Boston Evening Post,* June 15, 1782; *Continental Journal,* June 20, 1782; *Salem Gazette,* June 20, 1782; *Pennsylvania Gazette,* June 26, 1782; *Providence Gazette,* June 22, 1782.

[61] *Boston Evening Post,* June 15, 29, July 6, 1782; *New Jersey Gazette,* May 29, 1782; *Salem Gazette,* June 20, 1782; *Pennsylvania Packet,* May 25, June 11, July 2, 6, 13, 16, 18, 1782; *Maryland Gazette,* June 20, 27, July 11, 1782.

American diplomat or leader in Congress was mentioned by name. Aside from Washington the only other American to receive public accolades throughout the nation was Nathanael Greene. American republicans were awarding the laurels of victory and symbols of legitimacy to the men who were to rule them for the next generation. France was a monarchy but a "magnanimous ally." The references to the French, however, often implied that the aid and support of France were past. In the celebrations Americans wished the French well in the future, but few foresaw a close or lasting tie with their ally.

Members of the clergy played no conspicuous part in these celebrations, with the notable and understandable exception of Samuel Cooper. In part this reflected the growing separation of church and state, by which the clergy assumed a lesser role in society. The secular nature of the celebrations, not to mention the Revolution itself, is fully evident, although religious images frequently appeared in speeches praising the dauphin and the Yorktown victory. The ease with which Americans cast off one monarchy and saluted another is only a seeming paradox. Americans remained British in their orientation toward the monarchy and its functions. Charles I was still more controversial than Louis XVI in the American pulpit.

One religious organization did make a special effort to congratulate La Luzerne on the dauphin's birth. The Presbyterian Synod of New York and New Jersey called upon the French minister, and James Latta delivered the invocation for the occasion. News of this meeting and the speeches made were reprinted, but without any approbation.[62] Probably John Witherspoon, president

[62] *Boston Evening Post*, June 15, 1782; *Salem Gazette*, June 20, 1782; *Newport Mercury*, June 15, 1782; *Pennsylvania Gazette*, May 22, 1782; *Philadelphia Journal*, May 22, 1782.

of Princeton and a close ally of La Luzerne in the Continental Congress, influenced the synod in its decision to participate. The loyalist press was ungenerous enough to print what officials of the same synod had said about Frenchmen and the Catholic religion in 1766, which revealed more than a slight change in the organization's public pronouncements.[63]

Although La Luzerne was pleased with the response to his political tactics, he noted that Americans would go only so far in their support. The king of Spain was frequently ignored, La Luzerne noted, although that monarch had also aided the American cause.[64] In this conclusion the French minister was mistaken, however, because a majority of the celebrations did honor the Spanish king. La Luzerne had correctly detected the Americans' reluctance to acknowledge Spain's role. In part this can be attributed to the conflict between American and Spanish claims to Florida and the Mississippi River territory. Responding to intense pressure from France, Congress had reluctantly given up its territorial demands in 1779 in order to accommodate Spain. John Jay had been sent to Spain to negotiate an agreement, under instructions to compromise the boundary issues. Jay grew disenchanted with Spanish procrastination and revealed his discontent and growing distrust in his dispatches to Congress.[65]

Spanish-American conflict over border territories became a smoldering issue within the states and often in the Continental Congress. France had a signal advan-

[63] *New York Gazette & Weekly Mercury,* June 10, 1782.

[64] La Luzerne to Vergennes, Sept. 22, 1782, AAE, CP, Etats-Unis, 22.

[65] John Jay to Samuel Huntington, Sept. 22, 1782, Richard B. Morris, ed., *John Jay: The Making of a Revolutionary* (New York, 1975), pp. 825–35.

tage in that none of its territorial aspirations conflicted with those of the United States, which could not be said of either the British or the Spanish. The sentiment in favor of France and against Spain simply indicated that Americans would not willingly concede rights to territory that they believed should belong to the future United States. In retrospect we see that one of the strongest bonds of the alliance was French renunciation in the treaties of 1778 of any territory on the North American continent.

The celebrations of the dauphin's birth reveal American acceptance of the alliance, particularly following its success. But they also show rapidly diverging interpretations of the alliance and its future. The Revolution was often described as the beginning of a new age. Liberty, freedom, and independence had been secured as rights, and Americans proclaimed the need for these rights to spread throughout the world. In Hartford, Louis XVI received thanks for being the "supporter of the rights of human nature," while at Worcester the "friends of America throughout the globe" were saluted. At Trenton, Americans called upon every "friend of liberties in his country and the rights of mankind to observe the joy" of the dauphin's birth. At the Fishkill festivities the hope was advanced that American independence would "give freedom and peace to the world." One toast in Boston best captures the optimistic feeling of Americans in 1782. They proclaimed, "We feel Free —we carry everywhere a Consciousness of Freedom."[66]

This consciousness of freedom became the theme of the Harvard commencement in 1782, itself an exercise in revolutionary fervor. A student dialogue presented comparisons of the struggle for liberty in the republics of Switzerland, Holland, and the United States, a sub-

[66] *Connecticut Courant*, June 4, 1782; *Continental Journal*, Nov. 22, 1781; *New Jersey Gazette*, June 12, 1782; *Boston Evening Post*, July 6, 1782.

ject familiar to educated Americans. Richard Codman, a graduating senior, argued that the United States had many advantages over Switzerland and Holland because of the small American population and "our great extent of territory." The expected population increase would cause the American Revolution to influence "the liberties of mankind in present and future generations." This style of rhetoric was not unexpected at commencement exercises, but the audience's loudest applause came for Codman's description of "our generous and magnanimous Ally, the King of France, for arduously asserting and defending our liberties, and of consequence the liberties of mankind."[67]

This description of Louis XVI stands in marked contrast with many Frenchmen's views of the same monarch less than a decade later. Americans applauded his defense of the Protestant religion, of freedom of religion, assembly, and commerce, and of republicanism. Most of all, they praised Louis XVI for helping them defeat Great Britain. French society was soon torn asunder by groups seeking a limited provision of the very rights Americans cherished, thus making some of the claims for Louis XVI seem illusory, if not ignorant. For a monarch to defend the rights of mankind in the United States and deny these same rights in France offered only a seeming contradiction to Americans in 1782. Independence promised Americans a continuation and expansion of their rights and freedoms. Although they hoped liberty would spread through the world, Americans rarely lost sight of the centrality of the Revolution as an American experience for American freedoms and institutions. Beneath the euphoria over the Yorktown victory and the birth of the dauphin lay an inescapable truth: independence had been secured. Louis XVI had greatly aided the Americans in

---

[67] *Continental Journal,* July 25, 1782.

achieving this goal, and they could openly acknowledge his assistance without a searching examination of their own anti-Catholic or anti-French views. Loyalists might note the hypocrisy but to little avail, because the over-riding aim of an independent republic had been won.

The alliance between an ancient monarchy and an infant republic brought victory to the rebels of 1776. An undercurrent in the celebrations of 1782 suggests an uneasiness that Americans felt about their first entry into international politics. They had engaged in a strug-gle with the British Empire and its supporters in the United States, and with French aid they had gained vic-tory. But the victory had been a costly one, for a sizable number of Americans chose to live in exile rather than under the new government. The bright hopes of coop-eration among Americans faded before the reality of a Congress that was discredited and a financial structure that was severely damaged. Neither the Congress nor the state governments could control the rioters or wholesale evasion of the law in the following few years. The celebrations for the dauphin offered a demonstra-tion that victory had been won. But it soon became ap-parent that another struggle lay ahead as Revolutionary leaders tried to consolidate their positions of power within the United States.

That American support for France and Louis XVI had been limited would become fully evident in just a few years. Americans had started to deny the validity of the alliance long before the renewal of the British-French wars in 1793.[68] Louis XVI's fall from power early in the French Revolution served to remind Amer-icans of the perpetual uncertainty of a monarchy and the precariousness of rights that it guaranteed. A king

[68] William C. Stinchcombe, "L'alliance franco-americaine apres l'Independance," Jean Viguerie, ed., *Le Regne de Louis XVI et la Guerre d'Independance americaine* (Dourgne, 1977), pp. 125–33.

was a good ruler only as long as the public welfare was protected. When Louis XVI failed to serve this end, he found little support in the United States, and Americans showed small regret at his fate. Americans had accepted a curious mixture of political-religious history in which Charles I, then George III, and finally Louis XVI figured as parts of a larger problem.[69] In the peace celebrations of 1783, Americans looked outwards as they proclaimed that "the protestant religion shall prevail and flourish through all nations," while inwardly they cherished the hope that America would become "an asylum for the oppressed from all parts of the world."[70] This was the standard by which Americans judged Louis XVI and the French alliance.

The celebrations of 1781 and 1782 show us how far Americans had come in acknowledging the influence of the European world on their own affairs, in contrast to the narrow isolationism of 1774 and 1775. But the celebrations also reveal how rapidly Americans were defining their character and government in contradistinction to the rest of the world. In 1782 their vision of the future foretold a republic led by a new elite, an elite allowing a large role for the Revolution's victorious generals. This was to be a republic including both deference and slavery. It was to be a republic in which ancient rights were preserved and new rights extended. But primarily it was to be the Americans' own republic. The creation of this republic was the French alliance's most enduring monument.

[69] See H. Trevor Colbourn, *The Lamp of Experience* (New York, 1974); Felix Gilbert, *The Beginnings of American Foreign Policy* (New York, 1965).

[70] *Maryland Gazette*, June 12, 1783; *Boston Evening Post*, May 31, 1783.

JONATHAN R. DULL

France and the American Revolution Seen as Tragedy

I DO NOT wish to rain on the parade. The 200th anniversary of the Franco-American alliance is rightly a cause for celebration. Without the help of France it seems most unlikely that the newborn United States could ever have achieved more than a compromise peace settlement with Great Britain. Even had the new republic avoided actual extinction, to drive the British from bases like New York was beyond its military power. The achievement of such complete victory long appeared beyond even the combined capacity of France and the United States. Before the Battle of Yorktown the prospects of total British evacuation of the United States seemed remote. Despite their genuine commitment to American independence, French statesmen in early 1781 were forced to consider the danger that the war would end in a compromise peace, leaving Britain

I would like to note the assistance of my colleagues on *The Papers of Benjamin Franklin* and thank them for their critical reading of my text.

partial sovereignty or a part of American territory.[1]
From what we now know of Washington's hungry, un-
paid, and rebellious army, such pessimism was realistic.
Even the great French and American triumph at Yorktown fell well short of total and decisive victory. Britain
still held a number of important and virtually impregnable positions. Admittedly, Parliament finally lost hope
of reconquering the former colonies from these bases;
the Battles of Concord, Bunker Hill, Trenton, Saratoga,
and Yorktown had progressively undermined British
confidence in military coercion. Britain nevertheless
might have continued with ease to hold Charleston,
Savannah, and New York hostage. The decision to
abandon them and to concede American independence
was dictated in large part by the requirements of a
continuing war against France, Spain, and the Netherlands.

The Revolutionary War produced incalculable consequences for both partners in the Franco-American
alliance. For the United States victory in the Revolution
permitted the continuation of an experiment in self-
government now entering its third century. For France
the American war proved, ironically, a major cause of
political and social change. The French participation in

[1] France, Archives du Ministère des Affaires Etrangères, Correspondance Politique (hereafter cited as AAE, CP), Angleterre, Supplement, 19:216–23, untitled memoir of February 1781. For further
comment on the context of this memoir, see Jonathan R. Dull, *The
French Navy and American Independence: A Study of Arms and Diplomacy,
1774–1787* (Princeton, 1975), pp. 213–14. For French reluctance to
see Britain retain American territory see the comte de Vergennes,
French foreign secretary, to the comte de Montmorin, French ambassador to Spain, AAE, CP, Espagne, 593:247–48. For Vergennes's
commitment to American independence and the basis of his American policy in diplomatic considerations rather than mere commercial advantage, see Vergennes to Montmorin, Dec. 13, 1777, and
Mar. 17, 1778, AAE, CP, Espagne, 587:194–95 and 588:387–91.

the war drove the monarchy into bankruptcy. This made possible, although not inevitable, a revolution that ended the combination of absolutism, seigneurial privilege, and established religion called the Ancien Régime. I believe that both revolutions in the long run have benefited not only their countries of origin but also other countries that have found in them a model and a challenge. Rather than disputing either the significance or the ultimate benefits of French participation in the American Revolution, I wish instead to explain the nature of that participation. If we as citizens can find cause for celebration in a particular event, we as historians, either amateur or professional, must search that event for meaning. In this capacity, to see only the glory of the French participation provides meager benefits. We must search deeper to find material for reflection, for understanding, for legitimate historical analogy. I believe the French participation in the American Revolution yields its deepest meaning when seen as tragedy.

I use the words *tragedy* and *tragic* in three different senses. First, I use them as defined by the historian Bernard Bailyn in his study of Massachusetts Governor Thomas Hutchinson.[2] In justifying a new study of Hutchinson and of loyalism in the American Revolution, Bailyn expressed his view that the interpretation of great public events itself goes through different stages or generations. The first generation of historians of such events sees them in terms of heroes and villains. The successors of these early historians eventually find such explanations simplistic and search instead in the historical events for the origins of their own world and a justification of their own system of values. Eventually, however, a still later generation acquires the distance

[2] Bernard Bailyn, *The Ordeal of Thomas Hutchinson* (Cambridge, Mass., 1974), pp. viii–ix. Bailyn himself credits this interpretation of historiography to Sir Herbert Butterfield.

necessary to see great events as "tragic," that is, as fated by circumstance. From such a distance the bearers of disaster, the historical "losers" like Hutchinson, are seen not as villains or as object lessons but as men imprisoned by the necessities of their situation and by their own limitations. In this sense of the word *tragic*, so similar to the notion of tragedy in Greek drama, I propose to speak of the chief French participant in our Revolution, Charles Gravier, comte de Vergennes, Louis XVI's secretary of state for foreign affairs from 1774 to 1787. Vergennes has long reminded me of the protagonist in a Greek tragedy—a man both great and good, yet flawed, who inadvertently brings about the destruction of all he holds most dear.[3]

For the second sense of the word *tragedy* I propose to treat the French participation as an event of incalculable cost to the French participants themselves. Perhaps understandably there has been a reluctance during the bicentennial celebrations to discuss the costs of the American Revolution. First were the familiar costs of war to its victims. We have made our ritual gestures to the memory of the dead, but there has been an antiseptic quality to the bicentennial observances, rather like the antiseptic quality of death on television. However painful, I think it is necessary to reflect at times on how very unantiseptic it is to die from gangrene or dysentery or of malnutrition aboard a prison ship. Germans and Spaniards and Frenchmen and Englishmen and Americans, both patriot and loyalist, died such deaths, leaving wives and parents and children, often in great misery. We should reflect on them lest we love war too much, particularly a war with short casualty lists and a successful outcome. There were other costs Americans paid on

[3] The best introduction to Vergennes is Orville T. Murphy, "Charles Gravier de Vergennes: Portrait of an Old Regime Diplomat," *Political Science Quarterly* 83 (1968): 400–418.

which we do not dwell. There was the cost of losing tens of thousands of generally idealistic Americans who chose the wrong side and eventually became exiles in Canada or the West Indies or Britain. There were cultural costs, too, of suddenly cutting ourselves off from a great and vibrant culture; if we gained greater opportunities to develop a new culture, we paid a price as well, including the price of awkwardness and defensiveness and arrogance toward older cultures. Ironically, our victory itself may have entailed the highest cost. Only very recently have we begun to realize the cost of believing ourselves morally superior to others, invincible in war, God's chosen children—illusions stemming not so much from the Revolution itself as from the false lessons we learned from its fortunate conclusion.

If the costs of the Revolution to the United States were heavier than we care to recognize, the costs to France of her participation in that war were even heavier: not only the usual costs of war but also bankruptcy and the subsequent rending of her entire political and social fabric. That the French Revolution on balance proved beneficial should not obscure the fact that France suffered wounds far more severe than any endured by the United States. What seems most moving to me is that these wounds were borne above all by the leaders who, whatever their failings, were largely responsible for American independence. Vergennes had the good fortune to die in 1787, a few weeks before the Assembly of Notables convened, but most others were not so fortunate. Some, like Admiral d'Estaing, who brought the first French fleet to America, died on the guillotine; others, like Lafayette, suffered prison, exile, or both.

My third use of *tragic* perhaps is equally painful to contemplate. Although indispensable to American victory, the French participation was a mistake for France, a failure of tragic dimensions. Its benefits to France were illusory, its victories hollow, its accomplishments pointless. Born of misconceptions, only good fortune prevented its ending in military catastrophe. We may justly celebrate the French as brave and faithful allies, but to learn from them we must see their participation in another people's war as totally misguided—even though with Gallic good sense they were perceptive enough at least to pick the winning side.

Why did the tragedy occur?

Historians viewing the France of the mid-1770s now can see with hindsight France's impending internal crisis. The Ancien Régime had less than a generation of life remaining. The monarchy repeatedly had shown itself incapable of political or social reform. The weight of the state and of a society based on privilege and injustice fell ever more heavily on a peasantry hard pressed by inflation and overpopulation. The seemingly impregnable position of the nobility atop that society depended in fact on the support of the state and on the tacit alliance of nobility and wealthy bourgeoisie in defense of property. The nobility of course did not share our realization of their danger. The comte de Ségur, who had served in America, would reminisce, "We walked gaily over a carpet of flowers which concealed from us an abyss."[4] What the French nobility did feel in the 1770s was a sense of national humiliation. Many historians have described the American war as France's revenge for the loss of Canada fifteen years earlier. For some French noblemen, such as Lafayette (whose father had been killed by the English), there certainly was a desire for revenge, although revenge was often mixed with a desire for employment, glory, or profit. Such an

---

[4] Louis Philippe, comte de Ségur, *Mémoires ou souvenirs et anecdotes,* 3 vols. (Paris, 1824), 1:25. All translations are mine.

explanation, however, does not do credit to the motives of the French foreign secretary, the comte de Vergennes, who led France into the war.

Vergennes was born in 1719, the son of a president of the Parlement of Dijon and the nephew of a diplomat who provided his first professional training. Unlike most of his fellow noblemen, he had dedicated his entire adult life to serving the crown. After a decade's apprenticeship in Portugal and Germany as secretary for his uncle, Vergennes received his first post in 1750 as minister to the Archbishopric of Trier. His skill in Trier and in missions to the Congress of Hanover and to the Palatinate won him a major post: minister plenipotentiary and then ambassador to the Ottoman Empire, where he served from 1755 to 1768. He was recalled on the eve of the Turkish war against Russian expansion he had been ordered to provoke by his foreign minister, the duc de Choiseul; not until the dismissal of Choiseul at the end of 1770 was he given another position. From 1771 to 1774 Vergennes was ambassador to the Swedish court, where he helped engineer the coup d'etat of August 1772 that restored the power of the Swedish monarchy. In May 1774 Louis XV died and was succeeded by his nineteen-year-old grandson, Louis XVI. The following month Vergennes was named secretary of state for foreign affairs, largely through the influence of the comte de Maurepas, the new king's chief advisor (and surrogate father). Vergennes had already spent more than thirty years in diplomacy; he would be foreign minister for almost thirteen years.[5]

Although Vergennes was socially conservative, obviously his life-style and personality were hardly those

[5] For a detailed account of Vergennes's early career, see Louis Bonneville de Marsagny, *Le Chevalier de Vergennes: Son ambassade à Constantinople* (Paris, 1894) and *Le Comte de Vergennes: Son ambassade en Suède* (Paris, 1898).

of an eighteenth-century French nobleman. Fanatically hardworking, grave in manner, dedicated to his profession (as well as to his wife and children), he seems at first glance more typically a bourgeois. In important respects, however, Vergennes shared the mental narrowness and class snobbery of his fellow aristocrats. In particular he was almost totally ignorant of two vital subjects—economics and parliamentary politics. This ignorance would lead to disastrous consequences and doom Vergennes's diplomacy to sterility in spite of his idealism, dedication, and matchless knowledge of European diplomacy.

What ideals did he serve? Vergennes was not a philosopher and never explained the theoretical basis of his diplomacy. Three ideals, however, apparently motivated him: service to his king, concern for his country's security, and a sincere desire for peace.[6] Ironically, he undermined all three by needlessly involving his king and country in war. What could have led this peaceful man to mastermind a policy based on involvement in a foreign war? Fear. From the beginning of his tenure as foreign secretary in 1774, Vergennes was afraid for his country, even though at the time Europe was at peace and France in particular needed have no immediate fear of war. He was afraid because France seemed to be losing its position in the European balance of power, its ability to affect European diplomacy.[7] The Treaty of Paris of 1763, with the humiliation of losing Canada,

[6] Vergennes later wrote that the function of France should be to protect the public order (i.e., of states) and to prevent the equilibrium of Europe being destroyed (Vergennes to Louis XVI, Mar. 29, 1784, France, Archives du Ministère des Affaires Etrangères, Mémoires et Documents [hereafter cited as AAE, MD], France, 587:210).

[7] For a retrospective view of France's position in 1774, see Vergennes to Louis XVI, c. Jan. 1781, AAE, MD, France, 446:330–37 and 351–57.

contributed to that fear; Britain, moreover, kept the wound open by continuing to treat France with contempt. Bad relations with Britain, however, were nothing new, and in the intervening years France had pulled off a diplomatic coup more than counterbalancing her loss of Canada—the acquisition of Corsica. Of far greater consequence to diplomats like Vergennes was a diplomatic catastrophe seldom associated with the events of the American Revolution. In 1772 Austria, Russia, and Prussia collectively dismembered Poland, taking from her a fifth of her population and a quarter of her territory. What most appalled Vergennes about the partition of Poland was the way it broke the diplomatic rules. What in theory and surprisingly often in practice kept Europe from diplomatic anarchy was the operation of the balance of power, the governing mechanism of eighteenth-century diplomacy. Since in the eighteenth century there were generally about five major balancing powers, this system of mutual jealousy usually could be made to work, wars remained fairly limited, and the map of Europe did not greatly alter.

In 1772 the operation of the balance of power suddenly changed. Three powerful states (Russia, Austria, and Prussia) rather than thwarting each other's ambitions combined to divide the territory of Poland, a weak state. For a peaceful, conservative statesman like Vergennes this violation of the rules was a moral outrage.[8]

---

[8] At the time of the Polish partition Vergennes was restricted to the task of keeping Sweden out of war with Russia (Marsagny, *Le Comte de Vergennes,* pp. 315–18). Later, however, he would write bitterly of the Polish partition, "If force is a right, if convenience is a title, what henceforth will be the security of states?" (untitled memoir, December 1774, Archives Nationales [hereafter cited as A.N.], K 164, no. 3³. This document is quoted in Henri Doniol, *Histoire de la participation de la France à la établissement des Etats-Unis d'Amérique,* 5 vols. [Paris, 1886–92], 1:14–20). The greatest critique of Ancien

Even worse, for an experienced diplomat it was a warning of terrible danger to France because of the particular nature of the French alliance system.[9] Of the three great powers of eastern Europe that had divided Poland, France was allied only with Austria. French statesmen generally disliked and mistrusted Austria more than any other power on the Continent, and the major functions of the alliance were to restrain her and to prevent her allying with Britain.[10] The partition of Poland demonstrated that the Austrian alliance had become a dead letter, and France would soon confirm it by remaining neutral during the crisis of 1778 between Austria and Prussia. Lacking a reliable ally among the great powers. France was thrown back on a second line of alliances. Since the time of Cardinal Mazarin, France had been the protector of a string of client states that acted as a buffer for her—states like the minor German principalities, the Swiss cantons, and the Republic of Genoa. By the late eighteenth century these client states included several countries that were geographically extensive but militarily weak: Sweden, Spain, Poland, and the Ottoman Empire. This system of depending on several weak allies for want of a reliable strong one resembles the French alliance system after World War I, and it failed for much the same reason—France lacked the resources and the will to protect her friends.

Régime diplomacy is Albert Sorel, *Europe and the French Revolution: The Political Traditions of the Old Regime,* trans. Alfred Cobban and J. W. Hunt (New York, 1971).

[9] This system of alliances is described in Vergennes's instructions for the baron de Breteuil, ambassador to Austria, Dec. 28, 1774, given by Albert Sorel, ed., *Recueil des instructions données aux ambassadeurs et ministres de France depuis les traités de Westphalie jusqu'à la révolution française,* vol. 1, *Autriche* (Paris, 1884), pp. 454–500.

[10] Ibid. Vergennes once described Austria as "our ally in name and our rival in fact" (Vergennes to Montmorin, Sept. 21, 1779, AAE, CP, Espagne, 595:388).

Poland had been plundered while a humiliated France stood by. It was readily apparent from the weakness of the Turks and the aggressiveness of the Russians who would be next.[11]

As a former ambassador to Constantinople and Stockholm, Vergennes knew the problem well. France had enormous obligations without the resources to fulfill them, no reliable ally to help, and an uncertain amount of time until her diplomatic system deteriorated still further and her own security was undermined. There was, however, a possible way out. Austria, Russia, and Prussia had large armies but comparatively weak finances. If these states were cut off from subsidies they could not fight a major war. Only two states had economies developed enough that they could provide subsidies: France and Britain.[12] During Vergennes's youth the great French statesman Cardinal Fleury and the British prime minister Robert Walpole had cooperated to maintain peace and the status quo on the European continent. Vergennes considered Fleury his model and Fleury's time as a golden age of French security.[13] Thus the key to maintaining peace on the Continent was

[11] The problem of the Ottoman Empire is as constant a theme in the French diplomacy of the period as the Middle East problem has been in recent years. The most recent war between the Turks and Russians ended with the Treaty of Kutchuk-Kainardji of July 1774.

[12] Vergennes thoroughly discussed France's dire diplomatic situation in the memoir cited in note 8. He told the marquis de Noailles, ambassador to Britain, "Britain . . . is our first enemy, and the others have never had any strength or energy except through her" (Vergennes to Noailles, Jan. 17, 1778, Benjamin Franklin Stevens, ed., *Facsimiles of Manuscripts in European Archives Relating to America, 1773–1783*, 25 vols. [London, 1889–98], 21: 1839). Vergennes's colleague the comte de Maurepas claimed that the peace of the Continent had never been troubled except by British intrigues and British money (Doniol, *Histoire*, 1:284–86).

[13] Vergennes to Louis XVI, c. Jan. 1781, AAE, MD, France, 446:352.

obtaining the cooperation of Britain in restraining or at least not encouraging the aggressions of the eastern powers. The question was how to obtain it. The British looked on France with contempt; it seemed that only through a reduction of their power could they be brought to deal with France as an equal. The American rebellion presented France with just that opportunity to weaken the power of Britain. Here then, I believe, is the key to why France intervened in what in European terms was a British civil war. The American war was not for Vergennes a war of revenge; it was a preventive war fought to avert future catastrophe by rearranging the balance of power. Vergennes did not want to crush Britain; he merely wished to teach her some humility.[14]

[14] Vergennes described Britain as a necessary weight in the balance of power (Vergennes to the marquis d'Ossun, ambassador to Spain, Mar. 22, 1777, AAE, CP, Espagne, 583:426). This of course was also making a virtue of necessity—Vergennes realized that he would not be permitted by the other powers of Europe, particularly Austria, to crush Britain (Vergennes to the conde d'Aranda, Spanish ambassador to France, Apr. 26, 1777, AAE, CP, Espagne, 584:116; Vergennes to Montmorin, June 20, 1778, Sept. 21, 1779, AAE, CP, Espagne, 589:313 and 595:388). Active cooperation of Britain on the Continent of course represented the maximum for which Vergennes could hope, but even nonencouragement of the expansionist powers would be beneficial. I suspect that Vergennes's expectations varied according to circumstances. This was hardly a subject on which he could be explicit. Our most concrete evidence of Vergennes's desire for a rapprochement comes from a eulogy by one of his undersecretaries; see Henri Doniol, *Politiques d'autrefois: le C te de Vergennes et P. M. Hennin* (Paris, 1898), pp. 71–107, especially pp. 103–6. Hennin's testimony about his superior is supported by Vergennes's admiration of Cardinal Fleury, whose foreign policy depended on rapprochement with Britain and by the fact that, unlike his predecessor the duc de Choiseul, Vergennes was far more concerned with eastern Europe than with the maritime and colonial balance of power. It may be argued that Vergennes's policy toward Britain changed as a result of the American Revolution; I can see a change of tactics but not of objectives.

Even before the war was over Vergennes spoke of obtaining British help in saving the Turks from the Austrians and Russians.[15] The culmination of his British policy was not the Treaty of Paris of 1783, which stripped Britain of her American colonies; it was the Anglo-French commercial treaty of 1786, by which he hoped to tie the two countries together through trade, an eighteenth-century version of Nixon and Kissinger's Russian policy.[16] Note that in the armistice and the peace treaty ending the American war, Vergennes forced the British to agree to future commercial negotiations; these negotiations proved successful because Vergennes was willing to grant major trade concessions in exchange for minor ones.

There were three chief fallacies in Vergennes's British policy. The first stemmed from his total lack of understanding of French government finances. Preventive wars tend to become a contradiction in terms, and the American war created the very condition Vergennes fought the war to avert, a France too weak to be a factor in European diplomacy. The ramshackle and corrupt French tax system was too inefficient to fight the Amer-

[15] In a letter of late September 1782 Vergennes predicted that if peace could be reestablished before the end of the year France, Spain, and Britain together easily could check the ambitions of Catherine of Russia and those who wished to share them (Joseph II of Austria). "The three powers have an equal interest that the Turks not be expelled from Europe" (Vergennes to Montmorin, Sept. 28, 1782, AAE, CP, Espagne, 608:488–89). Lord Shelburne, the British prime minister, specifically encouraged Vergennes to believe that Britain and France might become the joint arbiters of public tranquility in Europe (Report of Gérard de Rayneval, French diplomatic envoy, to Vergennes, concerning Rayneval's conference with Shelburne of Sept. 13, 1782, AAE, CP, Angleterre, 538:156).

[16] The best account of the negotiation of this treaty is Marie Martenis Donaghay, "The Anglo-French Negotiations of 1786–1787," Ph.D. dissertation, University of Virginia, 1970.

ican war without massive deficit spending which so added to existing government debts that by 1787 the royal budget could not meet even the interest payments. The result was to cripple the monarchy both domestically and diplomatically. Turgot, the reformist finance minister, had warned of this in 1776 and fought his last political battle trying to convince the king not to give the Americans arms credits.[17]

The second fallacy in Vergennes's policy resulted from his failure to understand that in representative governments public opinion plays an important role in the making of foreign policy.[18] The attention of absolute monarchs generally had to be gained in a direct manner; after force or the threat of force had been applied, they could then be counted on to embrace a former enemy with a minimum of resistance and a maximum of hypocrisy. Popularly elected governments tend to prove more resistant to such sweet reason. The English country gentlemen who elected the House of Commons never forgave France for her conduct during the American Revolution. As a result Vergennes's policy was self-defeating. Britain did not become more willing to cooperate with France. Prime Minister William Pitt had great difficulty in gaining parliamentary approval for his commercial treaty with France in 1786; only the fact that the commercial treaty was so advantageous to Britain overcame parliamentary opposition. In spite of

[17] For Turgot's battle see Dull, *French Navy and American Independence*, pp. 44–49. Vergennes earlier had admitted to the king that internal reform was a prerequisite of a successful foreign policy (Vergennes to Louis XVI, Aug. 8, 1775, AAE, MD, France, 1897:45).

[18] Vergennes himself complained of the difficulties in trying to understand a government run by interest groups, "How does one establish even a calculation of probability where there is not even any fixed and acknowledged principle?" (Vergennes to Noailles, Oct. 3, 1777, AAE, CP, Angleterre, 525:56–57).

Vergennes's hopes it led to no real relaxation of mutual suspicions and produced no further diplomatic results. The treaty soon expired as a result of the French Revolution, but not before it had helped to produce a major depression in the French textile industry. Given enough time, it might have become as successful as the Anglo-French commercial agreement of 1861; in actuality it only demonstrated the futility of Vergennes's policy.

Vergennes was guilty of a third fallacy when he assumed that Britain would be seriously weakened if America became independent. Except for Adam Smith, almost everyone in Britain believed the same thing, so perhaps Vergennes should not be blamed too severely. He was, however, as ignorant of the functioning of the British Empire and the British economy as he was of the functioning of the British political system. He seems to have absorbed his knowledge of the British Empire and economy from the parliamentary debates and trade statistics his ambassadors sent him from London. He apparently did little independent thinking about such matters; his correspondence reflects the sort of jumble of received opinions and mercantilist assumptions to be found in a typical English country gentleman. In both Britain and France the same case seems to have been made for the importance to Britain of maintaining control over America, a case resting on roughly the following assumptions: The security of Britain depends on the strength of the British economy and of the British Royal Navy.[19] The economy and the Royal Navy are

[19] For Britain's dependence on her manufactures and navy for her position in the balance of power, see the memoir drawn up for Vergennes by his aide Gérard de Rayneval in March 1776, "Réflexions sur la situation actuelle des colonies anglaises et sur la conduite qu'il convient à la France de tenir à leur égard," reproduced in Stevens, *Facsimiles of Manuscripts*, 13:1310 (hereafter cited as "Réflexions").

dependent on the trade of the British Empire.[20] The trade of the thirteen American colonies is indispensable to the functioning of the empire.[21] Its loss would undermine not only the British home economy but the entire trade mechanism of the empire. Without the training provided merchant crews by the long voyages to America, the supply of trained merchant seamen would dry up and the Royal Navy could not find crews in wartime. In addition, the loss of the thirteen colonies with their naval bases and supplies would lead to the loss of the British West Indies.[22] (Unfortunately I have found no eighteenth-century reference to dominoes in this connection.) All of these dire results would follow the end of direct control over the colonies because the volume of trade was believed to be fixed and Americans were thought to trade exclusively with Britain only because forced to by the Navigation Acts.[23] Recognizing American independence would lead to a decline in British trade, the unraveling of the British Empire, and the loss of the Royal Navy's superiority over the French.

Arguments of this kind seem to have formed the basis of British fears and French hopes;[24] nevertheless, most

[20] A succinct statement of the connection between British power, industry, and trade may be found in Vergennes to Montmorin, Oct. 15, 1779, AAE, CP, Espagne, 596:81.

[21] This is expressed in Vergennes to Montmorin, June 20, 1778, AAE, CP, Espagne, 589:313.

[22] For the American contribution to the British navy and to imperial defense, see "Réflexions."

[23] See Vergennes to Noailles, May 2, 1777, AAE, CP, Angleterre, 523:6–7.

[24] An inflated sense of the indispensability of American trade seems also to have affected the delegates to the Continental Congress. They seem to have believed as well that because of the dynamism of the American population, American trade would become

of them proved false. The most conclusive demonstration that American independence did not harm Britain is the volume of British trade with America after the Revolution. By the late 1780s British trade with her former colonies had virtually regained its prewar level and during the 1790s surpassed it.[25] Perhaps this can best be explained as an example of what we now call "neocolonialism"; for more than half a century after the Revolution, America remained an economic satellite of Great Britain. In spite of the gloom shown by British politicians, the greatest period of British power still lay ahead in 1783. The British Empire, particularly in India, would soon expand; the Royal Navy would find ahead its greatest days of glory; and the Industrial Revolution, fueled by American cotton, was only beginning. In a very real sense Britain came out of the American Revolution a winner, France a loser.

Thus far I have discussed why France entered the American war. I wish now to discuss how France entered the war, how she was able to win her Pyrrhic victory, and how she finally extricated herself. The opening of the story is familiar enough—the decision of Louis XVI in May 1776 to provide a million livres of arms on credit to the Americans through a fictitious commercial company managed by the playwright Beaumarchais. This decision had been prepared by the visit of a French secret agent to Philadelphia, by petitions of Beaumarchais on the Americans' behalf, and by a considerable debate in the Royal Council of State in which Vergennes bested Turgot. This is the plot as presented

---

an increasing factor in the international balance of trade. See James H. Hutson, "Intellectual Foundations of Early American Diplomacy," *Diplomatic History* 1(1977): 1–19.

[25] Brian R. Mitchell, *Abstract of British Historical Statistics* (Cambridge, 1962), pp. 280–81.

in the standard histories; the only necessary change is the demotion of Beaumarchais from central character to subordinate player. I do think, however, that we need to reexamine the subsequent period, the period of limited French involvement in the war lasting from May 1776 to the alliance of February 1778. The decision to limit intervention at first to the providing of arms seems natural enough. If guns and powder for the Continental army were all that would be necessary for America to win her independence, then Vergennes could obtain his objectives with a minimum of cost and danger. In this connection I suspect that the eventual abandonment of the limited intervention policy was due less to the American victory at Saratoga than to the defeats at Brandywine and Germantown, which indicated that Washington's army was still incapable of defeating Howe on its own. Another reason for limiting intervention to the providing of arms was Vergennes's political position. He needed to approach so vital an issue as intervention with great caution so long as his rival Turgot wielded influence with the king and thereby political power. With Turgot's fall from office in May 1776 Vergennes had no remaining rivals in the making of foreign policy. He was a political ally of the king's chief minister, the comte de Maurepas; as long as his own primacy was acknowledged, Maurepas was willing to leave Vergennes control over foreign policy.[26] The young king was immature, lacked strength of character, and was ignorant of foreign affairs; Vergennes eventually obtained nearly total ascendancy over him on for-

[26] An example of Vergennes's deference to Maurepas is a letter of Vergennes to Louis stating that Maurepas was better qualified than Vergennes to suggest a new ambassador to the Court of St. James's (Vergennes to Louis XVI, Jan. 31, 1776, AAE, MD, France, 1897:56). Day-to-day direction of foreign policy was left to Vergennes.

eign policy questions. In May 1776, however, the king was still obsessed with the problem of royal finances, and Vergennes refrained from alarming him about the dangers in aiding the Americans.[27] Did Vergennes realize that the policy of limited intervention was likely to lead in time to war with Britain? No one knows, but I doubt very strongly that he had any illusions about the outcome. At any rate he was able to leave to Gabriel de Sartine, the French naval minister, the task of overcoming Louis's resistance to spending money and to leave to events the task of overcoming Louis's caution.[28]

The policy of limited intervention also made a virtue of necessity. Until the end of 1777 France was not prepared for war with Britain. The ships of the French navy needed repair, and French dockyards lacked the necessary reserves of timber, hemp, and masts. Since the navy would have to bear the brunt of war against Britain, its readiness was the prime determinant of France's policy toward Britain. During 1776 and 1777 this policy did not fluctuate according to news from America as most histories of the period indicate. Instead the progress of France from limited intervention to open warfare was fairly straightforward and can be measured by the number of ships of the line ready for service or by the cubic feet of timber in the royal dockyards. To understand the diplomacy of these years, it is necessary to trace the progress of French naval rearmament.

This interconnection of arms and diplomacy is readily apparent in reading Vergennes's diplomatic correspondence. Vergennes discussed naval affairs with his am-

---

[27] Note that the king was persuaded to adopt the policy of limited aid largely on the basis that it would *postpone* the danger of war (Dull, *French Navy and American Independence*, pp. 30–33).

[28] Ibid., pp. 49–83.

bassadors with a competence that belied his claims of being an amateur in naval matters. His predecessor Choiseul actually assumed the position of secretary of state for naval affairs from 1761 to 1766 (when he was succeeded by his cousin the duc de Choiseul-Praslin).[29] Choiseul had to rebuild a navy that had been crushed in 1759, a year of disasters including the defeats off Lagos and Quiberon Bay. The end of the Seven Years' War did not interrupt Choiseul's program of reconstruction; from at least as early as 1765 Choiseul planned war against Britain.[30] When the crisis for which Choiseul had planned finally occurred, Louis XV backed down. Choiseul and Choiseul-Praslin were dismissed and subsequently the stocks of war matériel were allowed to be depleted and the navy's warships to deteriorate. The most urgent problem inherited by Louis XVI from the last few years of his grandfather's reign, however, was administrative. A series of mismanaged administrative reforms had left the navy paralyzed. Louis's first need was a talented administrator; his choice, Turgot, quickly moved up to the even more critical job of restoring order to the royal finances and was replaced by the brilliant head of the Paris police, Gabriel de Sartine.

Sartine, although previously ignorant of naval mat-

[29] Choiseul and Choiseul-Praslin alternated both as naval ministers and as foreign ministers. Choiseul was foreign minister 1758–61, naval minister 1761–66, and foreign minister 1766–70; Choiseul-Praslin was foreign minister 1761–66 and naval minister 1766–70.

[30] Such at least is the opinion of M. S. Anderson, "European Diplomatic Relations, 1763–1790," in A. Goodwin, ed., *The American and French Revolutions, 1763–93*, New Cambridge Modern History, vol. 8 (Cambridge, 1965), p. 254. For a contrasting and, I think, less persuasive view of Choiseul's diplomacy, see John F. Ramsey, "Anglo-French Relations, 1763–1770: A Study of Choiseul's Foreign Policy," Ph.D. dissertation, University of California, Berkeley, 1935.

ters, proved highly competent in returning the navy to order. Two more intractable problems remained, neither soluble without large financial expenditures: the shortage of matériel in the navy's dockyards and the condition of the navy's warships. Sartine visited Brest, the navy's largest port, in August 1775 and warned the king that fitting out a fleet there would almost completely exhaust the dockyard's supplies and that upon the fleet's return it would be impossible to provide for its rearmament.[31] The major shortages were those of hemp, masts, and, most expensive of all, the oak needed for ships' hulls. To refill the empty dockyards would involve placing contracts from Scandinavia to Albania and would cost many millions of livres (by one of Sartine's estimates 18,000,000 livres, more than a normal year's budget for *all* naval expenses).[32] Sartine's success in obtaining royal approval in August 1776 for previously unbudgeted expenses was a major step in the evolution of French policy toward military intervention. By May 1777 Vergennes was able to predict that by the end of the year France would have on hand all necessary supplies for war.[33]

Proceeding simultaneously with the replenishment of matériel was the repair of the great ships of the line upon which war with Britain would depend. At Louis's accession the navy possessed sixty ships of the line with another four in construction, but none of these were on

[31] Dull, *French Navy and American Independence*, p. 26; for naval matériel see ibid., pp. 11–12, 21–24, 55, 66–68, and 82.

[32] A livre was roughly equivalent in purchasing power to between $1.50 and $2.00. The entire royal budget in 1774 was between 353 and 362 million livres (J. F. Bosher, *French Finances 1770–1795: From Business to Bureaucracy* [Cambridge, 1970], p. 90).

[33] Vergennes to Ossun, May 2, 1777, AAE, CP, Espagne, 584:138–41.

active service and all but twenty-four were in need of overhaul. Without extra funds no improvement was possible; by May 1776 only twenty-five were ready for service. With the need for protection for arms shipments to America and Sartine's success in overcoming the king's fiscal scruples, the number of ready ships of the line began to rise: thirty-seven by January 1, 1777, fifty by January 1, 1778. When France would begin war in the summer of 1778 she would be able to throw fifty-two ships of the line against sixty-six British—given the advantage of surprise, near parity.[34] The virtual completion of rearmament by the end of 1777 left France free to enter the war directly; there is even documentary evidence that as early as the spring of 1777 France was considering entering the war in time for the campaigning season of 1778.[35] The news of Saratoga, although opportune, was therefore probably a good deal less significant in securing French entry into the war than was the completion of rearmament.

In addition to rearmament and the progress of the war in America, there was a third element in the transition from peace to war. This was the tendency, familiar enough in other wars, of limited involvement in a foreign war to become progressively less limited. Gradually open war with Britain came to seem more and more inevitable. An informal coalition grew up in favor of war which combined intellectuals supporting American independence for ideological reasons, noblemen urging

[34] For available ships of the line see Dull, *French Navy and American Independence*, pp. 52, 66, 97, 351–53, and 359–60. Vergennes had predicted in January 1778 that because of her temporary shortage of sailors Britain would be unable to man more than sixty ships of the line for the war's initial campaign (Vergennes to Montmorin, Jan. 20, 1778, Stevens, *Facsimiles of Manuscripts*, 21:1853).

[35] Untitled memoir, n.d. but c. Mar.–Apr. 1777, AAE, CP, Angleterre, Supplement 19:308–10. For discussion of this document see Dull, *French Navy and American Independence*, pp. 84–85.

war out of Anglophobia and a desire for military employment, and businessmen who saw in both war and American independence the potential for profit. The sending of arms to America and the unsanctioned aiding of American privateers caused increasingly frequent British complaints. Incidents between French warships or merchantmen and British warships patrolling off the French coast became more and more common.[36] The growing support for war served Vergennes's purposes of course, but it also created the danger that war might be precipitated before the French navy was prepared. The worst threat of a premature war came as a result of the irresponsible actions of American privateer captains operating in European waters.[37] In August 1777 there occurred a crisis so severe that orders were sent to the French fishing fleet off Newfoundland to return immediately to France even if it meant leaving their catch behind.[38] The mounting difficulties of preventing incidents and of restraining martial ardor indicated the im-

[36] For examples see Port Commandant de la Touche (Rochefort) to Naval Minister Sartine, June 10, 1777, A.N., Marine B³ 641:161; Noailles to Vergennes, May 30, 1777, AAE, CP, Angleterre, 523:146–54 and following.

[37] A.N. Marine B⁴ 134 contains frequent letters to port officials urging greater vigilance against American privateer captains. Vergennes's mixed feelings are shown by this comment: "The Americans are instructed of our principles on that subject and I don't know but that it should have excited their discontent; it is to their dexterity and to their prudence to suggest to them the means of preventing their application" (Vergennes to Noailles, Mar. 22, 1777, AAE, CP, Angleterre, 522:135). Vergennes had taken a similar attitude in 1775 toward private (and illegal) powder shipments to America. Port officials were ordered to take precautions against illegal powder shipments but not greater precautions than against illegal shipments to places like the Netherlands; moreover, they were not to interfere with commerce (Vergennes to Sartine, Nov. 10, 1775, AAE, CP, Angleterre, 512:338).

[38] See Dull, *French Navy and American Independence,* pp. 75–83.

possibility of continuing indefinitely the policy of limited intervention. In July 1777 France began feeling out the position of her ally Spain on joint entry into the war before the 1778 campaigning season. At this time France urged that the decision be made by January or February 1778.[39] The arrival of the news of Saratoga in December 1777 therefore was perfectly timed. Benjamin Franklin and his colleagues began an elaborate charade to convince Vergennes that there was now the danger of a compromise peace between the United States and Britain. Vergennes immediately seized on Franklin's implied threat, although I find it most difficult to believe he was fooled for an instant by the implausible story that now that the Americans had won a major victory they might settle for something short of independence. Who was Vergennes trying to fool? I suspect it was both the scrupulous king, Louis XVI, and the Spanish foreign minister, the conde de Floridablanca, whom Vergennes hoped to lure into a joint alliance with the Americans.[40] Louis's reluctance for war was overcome, but Floridablanca, the toughest of negotiators and an astute statesman, was not fooled. Vergennes, upon abandoning hope for Spanish participation in the coming campaign, immediately began final negotiations with the Americans and signed treaties of alliance and of commerce at the beginning of February 1778. The royal council of state began final preparations for war, and hostilities began in June.

For the campaign of 1778 France had a great advantage in being able to choose when and where to attack

[39] Mémoire, July 23, 1777, AAE, CP, Espagne, 585:95–102.

[40] The Spanish government and particularly Floridablanca feared greatly American independence. Among numerous references is Montmorin to Vergennes, Mar. 20, 1778, AAE, CP, Espagne, 588:407.

and only a minor disadvantage in number of warships, since Britain was characteristically slow in manning her fleet. When the campaign ended without a decisive French victory, Vergennes was forced to purchase the help of the large Spanish navy by the promise of assisting Spain to recover Gibraltar. Why was the help of Spain so vital? France simply did not have the resources in sailors, matériel, or money to continue to match the British Royal Navy singlehandedly.[41] What eventually defeated Britain was a coalition of the American, French, and Spanish armies and the French, Spanish, and Dutch navies. This can be shown by comparing for each campaign the number of allied (French, Spanish, Dutch, and American) ships of the line in service with the number of British:[42]

Year	France	Spain	Nether-lands	U.S.A.	Total allied	Britain
1778	52	—	—	0	52	66
1779	63	58	—	0	121	90
1780	69	48	—	0	117	95
1781	70	54	13	0	137	94
1782	73	54	19	0	146	94

Only by applying pressure on all parts of the militarily overextended British Empire did France and her allies achieve the successful concentration of force at Yorktown that broke the will of Parliament to continue the

[41] See Vergennes to Montmorin, Aug. 15, 1778, and Feb. 26, 1779, AAE, CP, Espagne, 590:212–15 and 592:287–88.

[42] Figures for 1778–80 are ships in active service or fitting for service as of July 1; for 1781–82, as of April 1. All ships carrying fifty guns or more included; for the names and locations of each ship see Dull, *French Navy and American Independence,* pp. 358–76.

war in America.[43] On Vergennes fell most of the responsibility for holding the coalition together. The coordination of the military efforts of France, Spain, the United States, and the Netherlands called for all his diplomatic skill. Indeed, Vergennes provided the major directing hand behind the war and proved an excellent war leader. His balance of courage, common sense, prudence, and boldness were unmatched in the British cabinet, which took joint responsibility for running the war but which depended heavily on the inflexible and unpopular colonial minister, Lord Germain, and the strategically inept naval minister, the earl of Sandwich.

Vergennes had less trouble with the Americans than he did with the Spaniards or the Dutch since the war aims of the United States and France were both centered on the total independence of the United States. The achievement of that joint war aim, however, required Vergennes to take account of the war aims of his other allies.

The difficulty of coordinating war operations with Spain was apparent from the first. Spain's price for entry into the war included not only French aid in achieving Spanish war aims but also French acquiescence in Spain's dictating war strategy. Spain with her own overextended empire greatly feared a long war and hoped to win it in a single campaign. Before signing a convention regarding war aims in the spring of 1779, she extracted from a reluctant France an agreement to attempt the invasion of Britain. To attempt the operation, the allies assembled the largest fleet of warships in almost a century and briefly gained control of the English Channel. Unfavorable winds, sickness, and logisti-

---

[43] Vergennes specifically argued for the strategy of attacking Britain everywhere so as to keep her on the defensive and to find her weak point (Vergennes to Montmorin, Jan. 29, 1780, AAE, CP, Espagne, 597:219–21).

cal difficulties, however, prevented the sailing of the landing ships and the huge escorting fleet had to retreat to port. Vergennes, a realist about the difficulties and dangers of the undertaking, had been dubious about the invasion from the beginning and had sought to limit its scope. A successful invasion, moreover, would have had serious diplomatic repercussions on the Continent, perhaps even bringing Austrian or Russian intervention on Britain's behalf. Even before the fleet had returned to port, Vergennes wrote to Spain to urge a new strategy.[44] Not only was the invasion of Britain impractical but it was also a diversion of effort from America. Vergennes therefore urged that major efforts be made elsewhere. Since Spain could not afford by herself the enormous costs of invading Britain the idea was gradually displaced from allied strategy.

In the long run, however, the threat of another invasion attempt helped keep Britain on the defensive. The timid British naval minister Sandwich remained obsessed with the fear of invasion and kept enough ships in home waters to give the allies superiority in the Western Hemisphere. Although Vergennes was forced to let the Spaniards concentrate on their own military operations, he did talk them into combining forces for a short Atlantic cruise each summer to keep Sandwich distracted. Sandwich thus generally waited until too late to send reinforcements to the Western Hemisphere. The Spanish blockade of Gibraltar and attacks on Minorca and Florida forced the British to spread their resources still thinner. In 1780 the allies were able to send an expeditionary force to Rhode Island and vital reinforcements to the French West Indies and Cuba. At the end of 1780 Britain needlessly added the Netherlands to her

[44] Vergennes to Montmorin, July 23, 1779, AAE, CP, Espagne, 594:456–59; cf. Vergennes to Montmorin, Jan. 13, 1780, ibid., 597:107–8.

enemies. The following year the continual pressure finally forced the British into drastic mistakes that resulted in Yorktown. Shares of the credit for de Grasse, Rochambeau, and Washington's victory must go to a Dutch squadron in the North Sea, a combined Franco-Spanish fleet off the English Channel, and Spanish forces at Minorca, Gibraltar, Cuba, and Florida. It was due to this widespread pressure that the British lost naval superiority in North America and could not find the forces to regain it.

The results at Yorktown doomed the war government of Lord North and his colleagues. With the fall of the North government in March 1782 American independence was virtually guaranteed. Vergennes, however, had no time for self-congratulation. Britain abandoned the attempt to regain America the better to recompense herself at the expense of France, Spain, and the Netherlands. If 1781 was a year of victories for France and her allies, 1782 was a year of impending disaster. The crisis indeed was so severe that Vergennes proved willing to agree to a peace which gave France few gains but which extricated her from a terrifying combination of dangers.

The dangers, although interconnected, were of three types: military, financial, and diplomatic. On April 12, 1782, de Grasse was defeated at the Battle of the Saintes, near Guadeloupe, losing seven ships of the line. Although the defeat meant a postponement of the invasion of Jamaica, intended to end the war, the battle was not strategically decisive. As soon as the news reached Europe, ten new ships of the line were started in French shipyards. The news, however, was a warning of danger; the French navy had expanded beyond its resources in sailors and its morale had begun to crack. The captains of the French navy complained of the qualities of their crews; the new ship of the line *Pégase* abandoned a convoy she was to protect and surrendered after feeble resistance to a British ship of the line.[45] In contrast the British navy showed increasing aggressiveness and confidence.[46] Only the capture of Gibraltar or Jamaica could be decisive; with the failure of the Spanish attack on the former in September 1782 France was committed to another attempt on Jamaica. To capture it would involve one of the largest military and naval expeditions in the history of warfare. Half of the ships would be Spanish, most of them in dangerous disrepair. The campaign plans involved combining squadrons approaching from several directions in the face of a strong enemy enjoying an interior position. Even Admiral d'Estaing, the fleet commander, lacked confidence, yet to surrender the initiative would expose to attack the huge Spanish Empire and the rich French sugar islands. It was little wonder France delayed the start of the operation in the hope the peace negotiations would render it unnecessary.[47]

Hardly less frightening was the financial condition of France and Spain. All eighteenth-century wars were fought by deficit spending, and France and Spain had virtually exhausted their capacity to borrow money. French Minister of Finances Joly de Fleury estimated a deficit of more than 400,000,000 livres for 1782 alone; by the autumn of 1782 the navy was in danger of defaulting on its debts to war contractors.[48] Vergennes was forced to admit that France's financial means were ex-

[45] Dull, *French Navy and American Independence*, pp. 278–79.

[46] In a paper delivered at the Naval War College in April 1976, Piers Mackesy detailed this confidence of the British Royal Navy; I concur fully in his view that had the war continued 1783 would have brought the British victories to rival those of 1759.

[47] For the military crisis see Dull, *French Navy and American Independence*, pp. 299–301, 316–19, and 333–34.

[48] For the financial crisis see ibid., pp. 279–80, 297–98, and 345–50.

hausted and that Britain, by virtue of its constitution and its institutions, possessed financial resources lacking to her.[49]

The third crisis threatened to undercut the very objective for which France had entered the American war, the righting of the balance of power. The situation in eastern Europe had become increasingly threatening since the unstable and aggressive Joseph II had assumed sole control over Austria after the death of his mother, Maria Theresa, in November 1780. Joseph negotiated a secret alliance with Catherine of Russia in June 1781 aimed at the Ottoman Empire; although he lacked proof, Vergennes suspected the existence of the alliance and realized its target. He even predicted the point of greatest danger—the Crimea.[50] The Russo-Turkish peace of 1774 had left the Crimea an independent kingdom, subordinate to the Turks in religious matters but ruled by the khan of Tartary, who was a Russian puppet. In June 1782 the Tartars drove the khan from his throne; in spite of the Turkish desire to avoid involvement, Catherine now had an excuse for war with them. During the summer Russian troops entered the Crimea and Vergennes's representative in St. Petersburg warned of Russian preparations for war.[51] Unless France could extricate herself from the American war, she would be helpless to protect the Turks and

[49] Vergennes to Montmorin, Sept. 7, 1782, AAE, CP, Espagne, 608:317, quoted in Dull, *French Navy and American Independence*, p. 304.

[50] Vergennes to Montmorin, Dec. 20, 1781, AAE, CP, Espagne, 605:523–24.

[51] For the Crimean crisis see Robert Salomon, *La Politique orientale de Vergennes (1780–1784)* (Paris, 1935); Isabel de Madariaga, *Britain, Russia, and the Armed Neutrality of 1780: Sir James Harris's Mission to St. Petersburg during the American Revolution* (New Haven, 1962), pp. 409–12, 420–21, and 428–31.

prevent a European war. If French involvement in the American war was related to the partition of Poland, the termination of that involvement was related to the troubles in the Crimea—what better demonstrations of the Continental orientation of French diplomacy!

The peace negotiations of 1782 have given many generations of American historians the opportunity to castigate the French for duplicity. According to the standard interpretation, Vergennes conspired unsuccessfully to deprive the Americans of an advantageous peace so that the United States would continue to be dependent on France. This interpretation misrepresents Vergennes's conduct and totally misunderstands his motivation. Beyond total independence for the United States, Vergennes was not greatly interested in any of the issues negotiated in Paris between the Americans and British. He had sufficient worries of his own in finding terms to end the conflicts of France, Spain, and the Netherlands with Britain. His obsession was finding peace so as to avert impending financial, military, and diplomatic catastrophe. His major concern about the Americans was that they might delay the signing of a general armistice; ironically, they reached agreement with the British first without forewarning him. As justified as their action has seemed to subsequent American historians, the American peace commissioners came very close to undermining a general agreement between the other combatants. John Jay was even foolish and vindictive enough to urge the British to drive the Spaniards from Florida. Fortunately, however, Vergennes and the peace were rescued by the British prime minister, Lord Shelburne, who for his own reasons was as anxious for peace as was Vergennes. By the terms of the armistice and subsequent peace treaty, France, desperate for peace, obtained little for herself; instead she was forced to extract concessions for Spain and the Netherlands so they would agree to peace. The United States received independence, massive territorial concessions, and Newfoundland fishing rights, Spain received Florida and Minorca, and the Netherlands obtained restitution of most of their captured possessions.[52] France did avoid disaster, however, and Vergennes, overwhelmed by his last-moment rescue, attributed the deliverance to Divine Intervention.

What, then, were France's gains and losses from her participation in the American Revolution? In possessions she gained the Caribbean island of Tobago and the slaving posts of Senegal as well as the restitution of the island of St. Lucia, some commercial posts in India, and two small islands off Newfoundland. She also obtained the expulsion of a British commissioner from Dunkirk, the expansion of her fishing rights, and the promise of commercial negotiations with Britain. Small gains indeed for the expenditure of over a billion livres[53] (equivalent in purchasing power today to at least $1,500,000,000) and the loss of several thousand lives. The indirect gains for which she had fought the war were seemingly more substantial but proved ephemeral. Britain lost her monopoly of American trade, a small portion of which went to France; but, as we have seen, Britain did not take long to recover American markets and raw materials. Vergennes eventually obtained the commercial treaty with Britain he sought, but it cost

[52] When Vergennes's representative Rayneval asked Shelburne why he had granted the Americans boundaries all the way to the Mississippi, Shelburne mysteriously responded that it was part of his system, that he had found the principle of it in the works of Bacon, and that he would leave it to Rayneval to discover the principle (Rayneval to Vergennes, Dec. 17, 1782, AAE, CP, Angleterre, 539:365). For my own interpretation of the Anglo-American negotiations see Dull, *French Navy and American Independence*, pp. 324–29.

[53] Ibid., pp. 345–50.

dearly and led to no real improvement of relations. With Shelburne's fall from office Vergennes lost any hope of British cooperation in Continental diplomacy although Britain, by withdrawing into several years of isolation, at least did not work against him. Thanks in part to Vergennes's efforts the Turkish losses were restricted to the Crimea itself and during the four years between the American armistice and Vergennes's death in February 1787 this was the only major territorial change in Europe. Much of the credit for this stability belongs to Vergennes. If he was a force for war in America, he was a force for peace in Europe. During the thirteen years Vergennes was foreign secretary of France there was no general war on the European continent. This truly is the achievement for which he most deserves to be honored.

Vergennes was fortunate enough not to have to witness the costs of his policy toward the American Revolution. Within two years of his death his monarch would be bankrupt, France would suffer the humiliation of seeing another ally (the Netherlands) occupied, general war would break out in eastern Europe, and France herself would be on the verge of revolution. The French Revolution would develop its own momentum, and it seems extravagant to consider the course of events in 1789 as a consequence of the French participation in the American war. Suffice it to say that Vergennes, the most faithful servant of the Ancien Régime, helped prepare it for destruction, a destruction that eventually included the death of the king he devotedly served.

Perhaps the greatest tragedy lies in the alternative developments in Louis's reign that the American war precluded. War monopolizes the idealism, the energy, the financial and personal expenditures so desperately needed for the works of peace. Turgot was right when he warned that war would postpone perhaps forever the reforms so needed by the French monarchy. What if France had stayed aloof from the war, as she might have?[54] Perhaps kindly, idealistic Louis still would have been too weak and foolish a king to prevent eventual cataclysm. We shall never know, though, how long it might have been postponed and how many of its wounds might have been prevented. I find myself in danger of succumbing to sentimentality. Perhaps it is best to remain detached and admire the cunning of history which by bringing France into the American Revolution helped prepare the greater revolution to follow. We need not blink at the terrible injustices of the Ancien Régime or at the mistakes which underlay the French decision to aid the United States. As we celebrate the courage and idealism of our French allies, we can sympathize with their tragedy in spending that courage and idealism in the pursuit of illusions.

[54] That nonintervention was a viable option is supported by a letter of Louis XVI to his ally Charles III of Spain. While urging the necessity of military preparations, Louis admitted, "Perhaps there never has been an occasion when the appearances of a war with Britain seemed less likely; there is not the slightest dispute between us" (Louis XVI to Charles III, Aug. 7, 1775, AAE, MD, France, 1897:44). The same view is expressed in the comte de Guines, ambassador to Britain, to Vergennes, Aug. 7, 1775, AAE, CP, Angleterre, 511:156.). The same day these letters were written Vergennes approved sending a secret agent to make contact with the Continental Congress.

ORVILLE T. MURPHY

The View from Versailles

Charles Gravier Comte de Vergennes's Perceptions of the American Revolution

In March of 1795 Citizen Commissioner J. S. LeBrun of the French revolutionary government stood making an inventory of the possessions of the late Charles Gravier, comte de Vergennes. He examined some portrait engravings before him: one of Louis XV, one of Prince Kaunitz of Austria, and one of George Washington. All three together, Citizen LeBrun estimated, were worth no more than thirty livres. He jotted down the figure and moved on to a larger engraving, a map of the city of Constantinople. Methodically, he measured the map. Value? Sixty livres. Next Citizen LeBrun came to a copper plate of a portrait engraved by Vaugetiste. He counted the prints made from the plate and read the inscription on it: "Charles Gravier, Comte de Vergennes, Councillor of State Ordinary, Minister and Secretary of State and Chief of the Royal Council of Finances." The engravings showed Vergennes seated at his desk with a note addressed "To the King." The value of the prints, LeBrun decided, was thirty-six livres.[1]

Vergennes, diplomat and secretary of state under Louis XVI, entered the diplomatic service in 1739 as a secretary to his uncle Chavigny, at that time the French ambassador to Portugal. Later he served the French monarchy in Germany, the Ottoman Empire, and Sweden before he became secretary of state for foreign affairs for Louis XVI, or Louis Capet, as the French revolutionaries now called him. But in 1795 Louis was dead, his head severed from his body by Revolutionary Justice. Vergennes had known nothing of the execution of his master whom he had served for thirteen years. He had died six years before.

It would have been inconceivable to Vergennes at the time of his death that this upstart Citizen LeBrun, agent of the First French Republic, would be making an inventory of the objets d'art left by the comte to his oldest son, Constantine. Constantine, deprived of his titles and fortune by the Revolution, had fled the country to join the army of émigrés who were determined to return to France and crush the Revolution. Yet even at the time of Vergennes's death in February 1787 there were signs that the structure of the French monarchy was cracking. The state was on the verge of bankruptcy, the aristocrats were rebellious, and ideas of reform were circulating in the body politic. For Vergennes's unceasing search for rank, power, and order, pushed to its final limits, led to a self-destructive inversion: a collapse of power and then chaos. By performing his duties as he understood them, by being among the most responsible that his class and profession produced, Vergennes helped destroy the social and political world he served.

[1] Inventaire des objets d'art laissé chez M. de Vergennes, emigré (1793) Archives Nationales (hereafter cited as A.N.), F 17ᴬ (1268) 17°226.

Vergennes was an aristocrat; his life-style and work demonstrated many of the values of provincial nobility. His mode of life was not luxurious, he had little artistic taste or interest, and at court he stood out as an overly moral, very serious, hardworking servant of the king. Personally, he abhorred the extravagant, dissolute lives led by many of the court nobility. Yet, paradoxically, Vergennes's career shows a steady determination to raise himself and his family into the ranks of that court elite he detested. At Vergennes's death the family was ensconced in important diplomatic posts, his two sons were military officers, and one of them had been admitted to the king's exclusive court circle. The comtesse de Vergennes, although sometimes mocked because of her low origins, was nevertheless a prominent figure at court. Despite their relatively modest fortune and their social inadequacies; the Vergennes family climbed steadily upward during the eighteenth century.

But to see Vergennes only as an ambitious aristocrat would be to misunderstand him. He was also a professional diplomat, a career officer of the state, and a loyal and obedient servant of his king. As a high officer in the French Foreign Office, Vergennes belonged to an extensive bureaucracy that generated its own set of values.

Vergennes became secretary of state for foreign affairs in 1774, nearly thirty-five years after he first entered the diplomatic service. Most of this time was spent in service abroad. He knew international politics and the techniques of the diplomatic world as few other men in Europe. But he was a foreigner in his own country, so unaware was he of the many issues that divided Frenchmen over internal affairs.[2] "Rather than a Minister of Foreign Affairs," mocked the sarcastic Linguet,

[2] Vergennes to [?], Sept. 14, 1769, Documents originaux, no. 1. Bibliothèque de Versailles.

Vergennes was a "foreigner become Minister."[3] His ignorance of domestic problems and knowledgeability about world affairs explains a good deal about the failure as well as the glory of Vergennes's administration.

Louis XVI's choice of Vergennes to be his secretary of state was made, however, on the basis of the man's unquestioned experience and trustworthiness. Vergennes appeared to be the man who could help France regain a position of power and prestige in Europe.

England's growing problems with her American colonists made the times seem auspicious for France to assume once more a role that several generations of French monarchs and statesmen had felt was her special mission. The conception of France's place in Europe found its most straightforward expression in the instructions another secretary of state for foreign affairs, Bernis, gave in 1759 to Choiseul on his way to be Louis XV's ambassador to Vienna: "The object of the politics of this crown," Bernis wrote, "has been and always will be to play in Europe the superior role which suits its seniority, its dignity and its grandeur; to reduce every power which attempts to force itself above her, whether by trying to take away her possessions, or by arrogating to itself an unjust preeminence, or, finally by seeking to take away from her her influence and credit in the general affairs [of Europe]."[4] Bernis's idea had the unquestioning support of Vergennes. He had learned and absorbed it from countless instructions and dispatches he had received as a diplomat.

[3] *Lettre de M. Linguet à M. le Comte de Vergennes, Ministre des Affaires Etrangères en France* (London, 1777), p. 53.

[4] Instructions, Bernis à Comte de Stainville, 1757, Archives du Ministére des Affaires Etrangères, Mémoires et Documents (hereafter cited as AAE, MD), p. 42; Albert Sorel, *Recueil des instructions données aux ambassadeurs et ministres de France depuis les traités de Westphalie jusqu'à la révolution française*, vol. 1, *Autriche* (Paris, 1884), p. 356.

In a memoir to Louis XVI in 1774 Vergennes outlined his perception of this special place of France in European high politics.[5] France, he argued, should be the arbiter of Europe and the protector of the status quo. The second- and third-rate powers, he predicted, would welcome her as their guardian now that they had the recent example of the partition of Poland before their eyes. Happily, as the guarantor of the Treaties of Westphalia, France already had the authority to assume such a role.

Vergennes perceived the international system as a world of marked instability, of distrust and suspicion of friends as well as enemies, and of incessant competition among predatory states. In the midst of the instability, Louis XVI had to defend France, avoid isolation, and build the power and influence that tradition and personal character prescribed. To succeed, according to Vergennes, he must anticipate events by rational calculation of his interests, by reasonable deductions from facts, and by estimates of personal character. As Vergennes analyzed the political picture of Europe, he seemed to be demonstrating to the young Louis XVI an axiom he had once urged on his son, Constantine. Aside from the "impenetrable mysteries" of religion, he had written in a letter from Stockholm, everything should be submitted to the "tribunal of your reason."[6]

Yet it would be erroneous to conclude that Vergennes's notions of France's place in the international political system were derived purely from rational analysis. In another policy paper written for Louis XVI,

[5] Mémoire de M. de Vergennes à Louis XVI sur la situation politique de la France relativement aux différentes puissances, 1774, A.N., K164, no. 2². Unless otherwise indicated, all references to Vergennes's policies in 1774 come from this memoir.

[6] Vergennes to Constantine, Feb. 28(?), 1772, Archives de la Famille de Vergennes. For permission to consult these papers I am indebted to Vergennes's descendant, the baron de Thugny.

Vergennes, recalling the diplomatic situation in 1774, revealed that fear, vicarious ambition, aristocratic honor, and even personal ego were also ingredients in his perceptions of France's foreign policy. Vergennes reminded his monarch:

> Please remember, Sire, the position of France relative to the other powers of Europe when your Majesty took the reign of government and charged me with the Department of Foreign Affairs. The deplorable peace of 1763, the partition of Poland and many other equally unhappy causes had profoundly undermined the consideration due the crown of France, which in earlier days had been the object of terror and jealousy; [instead] there was only the opposite sentiment. Once reputed the first power of Europe, France barely had a place among the second-rate powers. Subjugated, after a fashion, by England, did we not see the ambassador of that power demand an account of our slightest moves, threaten us with war if we did not discontinue rearming begun in the Mediterranean and which we had to stop? Did I not, myself, watch this same ambassador in my office dispute Your Majesty's incontestable right to make civil repairs at Dunkirk and demand an explanation of the arming of your frigates for the purpose of training your navy? I confess, Sire, all the arrogance and insults against which my heart revolted made me desire and search for the means to change a situation so little compatibile with the elevation of your soul and the grandeur of your power.[7]

Vergennes's policy statements also reveal his own personal fatalism about the inevitability of war. War, or the possibility of war, was an element in every problem,

[7] Mémoire sur la politique extérieure de la France depuis 1774 adressé au Roi par le Sr. de Vergennes, 1782, AAE, MD, France, p. 446.

every calculation he studied. The longer peace lasted, the less likely it was to continue.[8] His view of the certainty of war meant that the priorities and resources of the state must always be prepared for it.

Certainly war was a constantly recurring theme of Ancien Régime high politics. Statesmen had to be ever alert for the surprise attack. And preventive war was by no means unusual. On the seas England had the reputation of attacking without a previous declaration of war. On land Frederick of Prussia held the dubious honor. But preventive war did not necessarily begin with a surprise attack on the enemy. The skillful monarch or statesman could provoke the enemy to attack and then call into effect the defensive provisions of his alliances. "[It] is easy to make a war without being, materially, the aggressor," Vergennes told Louis XVI in the spring of 1777.[9] Although he was speaking of Joseph II of Austria's relations with Prussia, his statement neatly summarizes France's policy of intervention in the American Revolutionary War.

Vergennes's conception of France as arbiter of Europe increased the possibilities for war. He defined the

[8] As early as 1774 Vergennes told Louis XVI in a memoir in which he recommended a buildup of French armaments that the longer peace lasted, the less likely it was to continue (Mémoire de M. de Vergennes à Louis XVI sur la situation politique de la France rélativement aux différentes puissances, 1774, A.N. K164, no. 2²). See also Vergennes's Considerations sur le parti qu'il convient à la France de prendre vis-à-vis de l'Angleterre dans les circonstances actuelles, Aug. 31, 1776, printed in Henri Doniol, *Histoire de la participation de la France à l'établissement des Etats-Unis d'Amérique,* 5 vols. (Paris, 1886–92), 1:567–77. Also Considerations sur l'affaire de colonies anglais de l'Amérique, March 1776, Archives du Ministére des Affaires Etrangères, Correspondance Politique (hereafter cited as AAE, CP), Angleterre, Supplement, 18:115–21.

[9] Vergennes to Louis XVI, Apr. 12, 1777, AAE, MD, France, 1897:77ᵛᵒ.

European balance of power so as to give France a superior position in the system rather than perceiving her as one nation among several who kept the system "balanced" because they were all relatively equal in power and influence. She was to see to it that the *other* states maintained an even distribution of power.[10] This role was, of course, the one Englishmen had, for generations, considered to be the prerogative of their country. In 1774, when England faced the necessity of withdrawing from Continental affairs, France became her competitor for the role of arbiter. The job of holding the balance of power theoretically required great self-restraint and a sense of duty toward others, especially the smaller, weaker powers. Vergennes recognized that obligation. Furthermore, he felt that in the Polish partition England had failed to meet her obligations. But he also recognized that to play the role of arbiter, France needed a margin of strength over other powers and some diplomatic advantages that she did not have after 1763.

Thus, in 1774 Vergennes was dissatisfied with France's international position, and he determined to change it for one more compatible with his view of Louis XVI's special role in the international system. In this sense he was a revisionist. Furthermore, he knew that England would not welcome France's bid to gain additional influence in Europe. England stood, therefore, in the way of France's becoming what Vergennes felt was compatible with the "elevation of . . . [Louis XVI's] soul and the grandeur of . . . [his]power."

Another factor in Vergennes's decision to go to war against England was a product of his long professional training. A veteran strategist, the diplomat had learned

[10] On this definition of the term *balance of power* see Martin Wight, "The Balance of Power," in *Diplomatic Investigations,* ed. Herbert Butterfield (London, 1966), pp. 148–75.

by experience to exploit the enemy's mistakes and embarrassments. For decades French diplomats, including Vergennes, had lived with the galling belief that England was the obstacle in the way of France's return to a position of authority in Europe. Now England, for a fleeting moment, was off-balance, exposed, and vulnerable. To the veteran diplomat with the reflexes of an old fighter, this was a unique opportunity. It was, as Vergennes said, the moment *le plus beau*.[11] His professional experience, his deepest instincts, told him he must strike; so he struck. The opportunity to inflict damage was a motive for doing so.

The American war fit into Vergennes's plans because it seemed to provide the right war at the right time. He shared with most of the other statesmen of his time the belief that British influence and power on the European continent was due to superior economic strength. And this strength, in turn, was in part due to her colonial empire, her foreign trade, and the Royal Navy, which protected both. If the thirteen colonies in North America could be detached from the empire, British power would be weakened because British economic prosperity, the colonial system, foreign trade, and naval strength were all mutually interdependent.[12]

The idea of breaking up empires to change the balance of power in Europe was not a new one; it dated back at least to the sixteenth century. By the eighteenth century, however, the competitive expansion of European powers overseas meant that the notion applied not only to Europe but to colonial territories throughout the world. In 1714, for example, the Treaties of Utrecht

[11] Doniol, *Histoire*, 1:570.

[12] On this aspect of Vergennes's reasoning see especially Jonathan R. Dull's discussion "France and the American Revolution Seen as Tragedy," this volume.

ending the War of Spanish Succession partitioned the Spanish Empire in Europe *and* overseas in order to rearrange the power balance on the Continent.

Vergennes's perceptions of the American war, however, contained several modifications of the tradition of partition. In the first place he did not intend to divide up the British Empire and parcel it out to other European states, including France. The American rebellion created, instead, the opportunity to separate a major segment of the empire from the mother country and establish an independent sovereignty under the guardianship of France. The final result, nevertheless, would be the weakening of Britain and a rearrangement in France's favor of the balance of power in Europe.

Vergennes understood that trade was a key factor in a nation's prosperity and power, and colonial trade was especially important to English power. But he also perceived that foreign trade with independent states could be as important to one's prosperity as trade with one's colonies. Vergennes's long experience as the French ambassador to the Ottoman Empire and the thriving, expanding French trade with the Levant impressed upon him that colonies were not necessary if the commercial advantages they brought could be acquired in another less expensive way.[13]

From the beginning of his administration Vergennes sought to increase French foreign trade without acquiring colonies. He first tried to gain more markets for France in the Spanish Empire and in Portugal. And it is noteworthy that in both cases the expansion of French

[13] On French interest in the Levant see Wenck, *Codex juris gentium recentissimi* (1735–1772), 3 vols. (Leipzig, 1781–95), 1:538; also "Mémoire de M. de Vergennes sur la Porte Ottomane," in Louis Philippe, comte de Ségur, *Politique de tous les cabinets de l'Europe pendant les règnes de Louis XV et de Louis XVI*, 3 vols. (Paris, 1801), 3:105–57.

trade was to be at the expense of English commerce. If France could get a larger share of England's commerce in Portugal and in the Spanish domestic and imperial markets, Vergennes felt, she could weaken England's international position.[14] Unquestionably he saw the commercial treaty with the Americans in the same light.[15] But whether it grew from foreign or colonial trade, commerce in Vergennes's eyes was always subordinated to high politics and the balance of power.

The American war also appealed to the French secretary of state's determination to prevent at all cost a war on the Continent when France challenged England. Previous wars with England taught France the danger of fighting a land war in Europe while at the same time responding to England's challenge on the seas. He recognized that France's role as a great power required more than the traditional French obsession with land forces. During the youth of Louis XV, Cardinal Fleury, whom Vergennes looked back to as his model for statesmanship, had given special attention to increasing the size of the French navy,[16] and Louis XV's secretary of state for the navy, the comte de Maurepas, had argued even more strenuously for increased French naval power. Like Vergennes, Maurepas saw England as France's most dangerous enemy. "I submit," he wrote to Louis XV early in the War of the Austrian Succession, "that it is principally on the sea that one must war on a maritime power." While agreeing that land forces were necessary, he argued, "Are not naval forces equally so

[14] Vergennes to Ossun, Sept. 13, 1774, AAE, CP, Espagne, 574:131. Also, AAE, MD, Portugal, Sept. 3, 1775, 1:294 ff.

[15] Edward S. Corwin, *French Policy and the American Alliance of 1778* (Princeton, 1916), p. 18.

[16] Arthur M. Wilson, *French Foreign Policy during the Administration of Cardinal de Fleury* (Cambridge, 1936), pp. 72–90.

when the war is against a maritime power?"[17] Vergennes's support of a French naval buildup and his determination to keep the war with England away from the Continent reflects the same kind of thinking. Was the idea really that of Maurepas, whom Louis XVI called back into his administration in 1774? It is impossible to say for certain, but Vergennes's respect for Maurepas's experience and his close collaboration with him and the secretary of state for the navy, Gabriel de Sartine, suggest an affirmative answer. Certainly their frequent meetings offered numerous occasions to exchange and explore such opinions.

Convinced that war with England was coming, Vergennes sought to delay it until the French navy was prepared. The longer the Americans held out, the longer France had to rebuild her navy. Vergennes's advocacy of secret aid to the Americans was intended to buy the time needed to build up naval strength. Despite his rhetoric about military strength being the best guarantee of peace, he was not building the French navy to preserve the peace but to win a war. Jonathan R. Dull's book *The French Navy and American Independence* leaves no doubt about the matter.[18] War did not occur before 1778, partly because the French navy was not ready for it. Veteran observers in Europe knew, however, that when France was ready, war became "more or less probable."[19]

From the viewpoint of classical diplomacy, the guid-

[17] René Jouan, *Histoire de la marine française* (Paris, 1932), p. 223.

[18] Jonathan R. Dull, *The French Navy and American Independence: A Study of Arms and Diplomacy, 1774–1787* (Princeton, 1975).

[19] The Danish envoy to Spain, St. Saphorin, to his superior, Bernstorff, Jan. 9, 30, 1777, AAE, CP, Danemarck, 161:13–13ᵛᵒ and 48ᵛᵒ. Also, Bernstorff to the baron de Blome, envoy extraordinary of Denmark, Jan. 21, 1777, ibid., p. 35.

ance Vergennes gave to Louis XVI during the crisis of
the American war was impeccable. It demonstrated the
secretary of state's understanding of international politics as well as his superb mastery of the techniques of
diplomacy. Nevertheless, it was based on a shocking
misunderstanding of domestic affairs, of the seriousness of the long-standing fiscal and economic difficulties
of the French government, and it ignored completely
the growing cry for social justice in France. Vergennes's
advice was limited by a professional and a class bias that
subordinated the most serious domestic problems to
foreign affairs. Vergennes left fiscal problems to others.
He apparently even allowed himself the illusion that
war would somehow help solve the problems of the
state debt because the king could impose extraordinary
taxes during wartime and his subjects would not
complain. When the controller-general of finances,
Jacques Necker, embarked on the dangerous policy
of trying to solve France's wartime financial problems
by the expedient of further loans, Vergennes was one
of his most enthusiastic supporters. "If he [Necker] can
end the war without straying from this system,"
Vergennes applauded, "he will be a great man in the
field."[20]

Preventive war was justified by diplomatic practice,
but Christian morality and aristocratic honor certainly
condemned deceit and an unprovoked attack on an
enemy. Vergennes personally appreciated this moral
position; he had eloquently used it earlier to argue

[20] Vergennes to La Luzerne, Mar. 9, 1781, AAE, CP, Etats-Unis,
15:341–44vo; Vergennes to Montmorin, Dec. 17, 1779, AAE, CP,
Espagne, 596:182; the marquis d'Argenson, *Considérations sur le government ancien et présent de la France* (Amsterdam, 1765), p. 18; on
Vergennes's idea that the war might help solve the problem of the
state debt, see his elaboration in Vergennes to Ossun, June 14, 1776,
AAE, CP, Espagne, 580:389.

against the Spanish king's plans for a preventive war.[21] His moral distaste for the Polish partition, Frederick's attack on Silesia, and England's unprovoked attacks at sea was sincere and reflected a deep personal repugnance for deceit and naked force as means in the affairs of men and states.

How, then, could he justify to himself and others an aggressive intervention in the American Revolution? Clearly he did so by viewing the decision as one of necessity, not choice. Since war with England, was "inevitable," there was no moral choice to be made. Peace, to him, was not a live option. Herein lies the essential difference in the perceptions of Vergennes and Turgot. If Turgot could have persuaded Louis XVI and Vergennes that peace, not war, was a necessity if the monarchy were to survive, the history of Louis XVI's reign would have been very different. But Vergennes never saw peace with England in this light. The area of his professional concern became, therefore, strategic: when and under what conditions could France best fight the war?

Vergennes deliberately provoked a war with England to recover for France a role in European affairs that had been presumably lost in 1763. Nevertheless, he took care that Louis XVI did not appear to be the aggressor. Personally, his own moral scruples opposed an open attack on England. Furthermore, the alliance with the Americans was a defensive one which came into effect only in the event that Great Britain "should break the peace with France either by direct hostilities, or by hindering her commerce and navigation."[22] It is not likely

[21] Vergennes to Aranda, Nov. 25, 1775, AAE, CP, Espagne, 578:257.

[22] Gilbert Chinard, ed., *The Treaties of 1778 and Allied Documents* (Baltimore, 1928), p. 51.

that either the French or the Americans would have quibbled much over whether a French war with England was defensive or offensive, since both governments wanted French intervention. Still, Vergennes wanted no room for dispute over the issue.

Moreover, diplomatically and militarily, Vergennes had nothing to gain from a French surprise attack on England. French aid to the Americans and the treaty of amity and commerce placed George III in an untenable position, since it denied his legal authority over the Americans and provided the means to resist that authority. Nevertheless, until the French publicly announced their treaty with the rebels, England preferred to overlook the intervention of France rather than precipitate open warfare.[23]

An attack on England would have activated England's defensive alliances and brought other European powers into the fray. The war would then no longer be confined to the American continent and the seas, and France would lose the strategic advantage Vergennes hoped to exploit. Moreover, Vergennes was convinced that Britain's allies would stay out of the war if at all possible.[24] French interests, therefore, required that England have no claim on her allies.

Perhaps Great Britain might have avoided even longer an open break with France if the latter, on Vergennes's initiative, had not presented to George III a diplomatic note formally delivered by the French ambassador which publicly recognized the independence of the United States and announced the signing of the treaties of February 6, 1778. The note was a deliberate affront to the British monarch before the eyes of Eu-

[23] Samuel Flagg Bemis, *The Diplomacy of the American Revolution* (1935; reprint ed., Bloomington, Ind., 1957), p. 66.

[24] "Mémoire," December 1777, in Doniol, *Histoire,* 2:160.

rope and it came because Vergennes felt France was ready to fight. Vergennes, of course, insisted that the note was not intended to provoke England to war, but other diplomats saw the matter in another light. The Danish foreign minister, count von Bernstorff, remarked that the French ambassador's note "was the signal for war."[25] Another diplomat said that the note made war "inevitable."[26] And a third, a French chargé d'affaires at Copenhagen, admitted that the note would be promptly followed by a British declaration of war.[27]

The fiction that England was the aggressor was important to Vergennes for another reason. When the crisis of the Bavarian succession developed, Joseph II of Austria ordered his troops into Bavaria and then asked Louis XVI to support him, in accordance with the Franco-Austrian alliance of 1756. France refused on the grounds that the alliance was only defensive and Joseph's act was an offensive one. Earlier, the French ambassador to Vienna had broached to Joseph the subject of Austrian aid to France if France were attacked.[28] Joseph was reluctant to commit himself. After the British attacked the French frigate *La Belle Poule,* Vergennes went to great lengths to convince the Austrians that the British were indeed the aggressors. But Austria would not agree to this contention.[29] Finally, Vergennes sug-

[25] Bernstorff to de Blome, Mar. 28, 1778, AAE, CP, Danemarck, 161:281. Vergennes to Breteuil, Mar. 10, 1778, AAE, CP, Autriche, 333:203; see also "Note" by M. Barthelemy, ibid., p. 216.

[26] Dieyer to Schultz, Mar. 31, 1778, AAE, CP, Danemarck, 161:181 vo

[27] Caillard to Vergennes, Mar. 31, 1778, ibid., p. 283.

[28] Breteuil to Vergennes, Apr. 17, 1778, AAE, CP, Autriche, 333:255–55 vo.

[29] Vergennes to Breteuil, June 22, 1778, AAE, CP, Autriche, 335:61–62; Vergennes to Breteuil, July 11, 1778, ibid., pp. 89–89 vo. The British naval historian William Laird Clowes concluded that in

gested that in order to prevent embarrassment the two allies ought to recognize each other's positions and not claim aid.[30] Throughout the Bavarian crisis whenever Joseph demanded help, Vergennes responded that France's right to Austrian aid in the Americas was equal to Austria's right to French aid in the Bavarian war. The response probably never convinced Joseph, but it blunted the effect of his demands on France. By maintaining the fiction that England was the aggressor, Vergennes persistently fended off Joseph's attempts to divert France's military efforts away from the American war.

Experienced diplomats were not taken in by Louis XVI's claim that England had aggressed against France. As early as 1776 European diplomats knew of Beaumarchais's comings and goings, they knew American ships were loading munitions at Le Havre, and that Vergennes and the British ambassador had clashed over the French interference in the British Empire.[31] The Danish ambassador to Madrid remarked in January 1777 that there would probably be no war that year because England was too busy with her colonies and France and Spain were not yet ready for it. But he accurately predicted that the developments of the coming year would make war likely.[32] The Danish ambassador at Versailles

the attack on the *Belle Poule* Britain was technically the aggressor but that the behavior of the *Belle Poule* and her sister ship was "so unfriendly" as to justify the attack (*The Royal Navy: A History from the Earliest Times to the Present,* 7 vols. [London, 1897–1903], 4:13 ff.).

[30] Vergennes to Breteuil, Aug. 20, 1778, AAE, CP, Autriche, 335:148–49[vo]; Vergennes to Breteuil, July 20, 1778, ibid., p. 102; Vergennes to Breteuil, July 26, 1778, ibid., p. 101.

[31] De Blome to Bernstorff, Dec. 19, 1776, AAE, CP, Danemarck, 160:487[vo] and 498; Bemis, *The Diplomacy of the American Revolution,* p. 65.

[32] St. Saphorin to Bernstorff, Madrid, Jan. 30, 1777, AAE, CP, Danemarck, 161:48[vo].

saw that the French were determined not to appear the aggressors in the war, but he also saw that the decisions being made to put the French navy in operational readiness were a "decisive" sign of war with England.[33] His superior at Copenhagen agreed. Bernstorff openly questioned France's attempts to demonstrate England's guilt for starting the war. France, he noted, wished to date the beginning of the war with the British attack on *La Belle Poule*. But England dated the beginning of the hostilities much earlier.[34] In Austria, Joseph II told the French ambassador the same thing. To Joseph the Franco-American treaty began the war because it made it "inevitable" that England attack France.[35] In his view the attack on *La Belle Poule* seemed only a skirmish in a war already begun by French action.

Vergennes's plans for war also entailed some unsuccessful attempts at deception. While he prepared for war, he tried to convince the British that Louis XVI did not seek to profit from England's embarrassment in America.[36] Later developments make it clear that Vergennes's statements to the British were blatant lies, but Vergennes continued to maintain the same official stance: France would not use the American revolt to embarrass England.[37]

Again, professional diplomats were not deceived. From the beginning of Franco-American contacts, British spies kept London informed of what was happening

[33] De Blome to Bernstorff, Mar. 15, 1778, ibid., p. 268.

[34] Caillard to Vergennes, July 28, 1778, ibid., pp. 296–98[vo].

[35] Breteuil to Vergennes, Mar. 24, 1778, AAE, CP, Autriche, 333:222.

[36] Vergennes to Guines, June 23, 1775, AAE, CP, Angleterre, 510:297–97[vo].

[37] Vergennes to Guines, Aug. 27, 1775, ibid., 511:317–17[vo].

at Versailles.[38] And even if the British spy system had been incompetent, alert English diplomats could have learned of the French deception from other European diplomats. The Danish minister Bernstorff followed in Copenhagen the course of French intervention step by step,[39] and from Madrid the reports of his representative, St. Saphorin, were amazingly accurate.[40] If the Danish diplomatic corps was so well-informed, the diplomats of other powers must have also been aware of the deceptions of the French government. Louis XVI knew this. When he tried to explain to Charles III of Spain why he signed treaties with the United States without full consultation with Madrid, he gave as one reason for his haste that French involvement was no longer a secret and the British were threatening to avenge themselves.[41]

If Louis really believed that the breakdown of secrecy brought England closer to an attack on France, did he not see, as Vergennes surely did, that a public announcement in London of a Franco-American alliance would provoke England to open war? The treaties of February 6, 1778, and the public announcement of them were Vergennes's way of beginning the war "without being materially the aggressor."[42]

---

[38] Samuel Flagg Bemis, "British Secret Service and the Franco-American Alliance," *American Historical Review* 29 (1924): 474–75; idem, *Diplomacy of the American Revolution*, pp. 65–66.

[39] Bernstorff to de Blome, Jan. 21, 1777, AAE, CP, Danemarck, 161:35.

[40] St. Saphorin to Bernstorff, Jan. 30, 1777, ibid., p. 48vo.

[41] Louis XVI to Charles III, Mar. 9, 1778, A.N., K164, no. 3.

[42] Vergennes to Louis XVI, Apr. 12, 1777, AAE, MD, France, 1897:77vo. In referring to Joseph II's diplomacy, Vergennes wrote to Louis XVI: "It is easy to make a war without being materially the aggressor."

In short, the Anglo-French war was a preventive war in which France played the role of provocateur, while trying to maintain the fiction that England was the aggressor. Vergennes evaded the moral responsibility for his acts on the grounds that they were determined by necessity, while Turgot argued that peace, not war, was the real necessity. The intervention demonstrates Vergennes's mastery of the techniques of international diplomacy. It also demonstrates his blindness: he could not appreciate France's domestic crisis or Turgot's warnings about the inability of the king's treasury to pay for his foreign policy.

The French intervention, therefore, required considerable deception on the part of a man who personally cultivated the reputation of being morally upright and honest. Vergennes did not deceive the veteran diplomats of Europe. But did he deceive himself? Did he believe that his actions were consistent with his personal morals? It is impossible to say. Certainly history shows that the argument of "necessity" is frequently used by statesmen to justify or to hide, from themselves as well as from others, the inconsistencies between their actions and the moral traditions they believe in. Vergennes's justification of his actions on the grounds of necessity smacks of this sort of self-deception. Whatever the case, he continued to cultivate at court the image of the honest, hardworking, Christian family man,[43] while he privately admitted to his colleagues in the field that the limits for what is permissible in "politics are not quite as strict as [they are] for morality."[44]

Vergennes's perceptions of how France could exploit

[43] Alexandre Tratchevsky, "La France et l'Allemagne sous Louis XVI," *Revue Historique* 14 (1881): 257.

[44] Vergennes to Monteil, Sept. 14, 1779, AAE, CP, Genoa, 160:330.

the war in America to better France's position in Europe were dependent, of course, on the reliability of American military forces. A professional diplomat, trained to calculate and measure power, the secretary of state naturally included estimates of armies in all his considerations. It was imperative, therefore, that he pay special attention to estimates of the American Continental army and the militia.

The Seven Years' War had barely closed before the American colonists began to object to the British attempts to implement the Stamp Act. The French secretary of state for foreign affairs at the time, the duc de Choiseul, sent several agents into England and America to gauge American strength and hostility to England. Choiseul wanted to encourage, if the time seemed ripe, a revolutionary movement in America. Choiseul was no revolutionary, but he had reached the conclusion that it was an error to fight England on the Continent. If she were to be defeated, she had to be challenged on the sea. And if Englishmen could be entangled in a conflict with their colonies abroad while the new French strategy was carried out, so much the better.[45]

The extent to which Choiseul tried to implement his plans is seen when we study the mission of Johann de Kalb, who visited America in 1767. De Kalb's instructions ordered him to investigate the attitudes of the Anglo-Americans and find out what military resources were available to them. The French agent was to learn the needs of the colonists for officers instructed in engineering and artillery, examine the colonists' potential for raising troops, find the locations of their strong points and entrenched forts, and even discover what

---

[45] On Choiseul's plans see "Mémoire pour le Roi," in *Journal des Savants* (1881), pp. 171–84, 250–57.

plans the Americans had for a revolt, including the names of those who would be their leaders.[46]

The character of the information sought by Choiseul underlines the seriousness of his project. De Kalb's reports, which concluded with the opinion that "the present condition of the colonies is not such as to enable them to repel force with force," played an important role in Choiseul's decision not to follow through with plans based on the possibility of a revolt in the American colonies.[47] By 1769 Choiseul's policy had been abandoned, but it was revived by Vergennes after he became secretary of state for foreign affairs. When Vergennes returned to Choiseul's policy, Choiseul's condition that there be an American resistance capable of sustaining itself appeared to be a reality.

We do not know whether Vergennes read the reports on the colonies written by the agent sent out by Choiseul. But one thing is certain: when he took over the office of foreign affairs, he had as his *premier commis* (undersecretary) Conrad Alexandre Gérard, a man who had worked under Choiseul and who knew well the details of Choiseul's foreign policy regarding America and England. The close collaboration that developed between Vergennes and Gérard offered many opportunities for discussion of Anglo-American affairs.[48]

As early as 1774 the possibilities for a French exploitation of the critical situation in America were pointed out to Versailles by the French representative in London. Garnier reminded his superiors that England could be forced into a position of a second-rate power if

[46] Vicomte de Colleville, *Les missions secrètes du Général Major Baron de Kalb* (Paris, 1885), p. 20.

[47] Ibid., p. 31.

[48] John J. Meng, ed., *Dispatches and Instructions of Conrad Alexandre Gérard, 1778–1780* (Paris, 1939), pp. 43–44.

she were compelled to expend all of her resources to bring the colonies under control.[49] Vergennes agreed that the "quarrel between the colonies and the British government appears to become more serious day by day." If the factions in America took on some consistency, he allowed, they could "deliver the most fatal blows to the authority of the mother country."[50]

Clearly, the French government took a cautious interest in the affairs of America. At the same time it recognized that the American resistance to England might be so fragile as to disintegrate at the first blow. Also, the French military was in no condition to sustain a war. Vergennes felt compelled, therefore, to assure the English, through diplomatic channels, that the Americans would be committing a grave error if they counted on the least encouragement from France.[51]

Vergennes's diplomatic decisions developed, therefore, with a careful sifting of estimates of the ability of the Americans to field and maintain a viable military force. In July 1775 he first began to realize that the American revolt reopened the options conceived by Choiseul. Guines, the French ambassador to London, wrote to him that it appeared possible that the entire British army would not be able to reduce the Americans to submission.[52]

But did the Americans, in fact, have sufficient force to carry through full-scale rebellion? Guines pointed out to Vergennes that neither London nor the French government knew very much about American capabilities, and he suggested that some reliable person be sent

[49] Garnier to Vergennes, Aug. 10, 1774, AAE, CP, Angleterre, 506:154.

[50] Vergennes to Garnier, Sept. 11, 1774, ibid., p. 263.

[51] Garnier to Vergennes, Dec. 19, 1774, ibid., p. 321.

[52] Guines to Vergennes, July 1, 1775, ibid., 511:12–12vo.

to take "a good look at the [Americans] politically and militarily."[53] Vergennes agreed[54] and sent Achard de Bonvouloir, a French army officer who knew America from previous visits, to gather intelligence for Versailles.[55] The new year, 1776, was not yet two months old before Bonvouloir's reports began to arrive at Versailles. The American military potential, Bonvouloir estimated, showed great promise. "Everyone here is a soldier," he wrote. "The troops are well clothed, well paid and well commanded. They have about 50,000 volunteers who do not want pay. You can judge whether people of this stamp will fight."[56] Bonvouloir's report confirmed information coming from other sources.[57] Vergennes was now more than ever convinced that the Americans could fight and had an army to do so. His policy recommendations in March 1776 to secretly aid the Americans demonstrated his confidence.[58]

Meanwhile, intelligence on the American army accumulated. By April 1776 Vergennes perceived a revolutionary army in America of 50,000 regular troops "well-dressed, well-disciplined and well-commanded."[59] The secretary of state concluded that the insurgents

[53] Guines to Vergennes, July 1, 1775, ibid., pp. 16–17.

[54] Vergennes to Guines, Aug. 7, 1775, ibid., p. 227.

[55] Joseph Hamon, *Le Chevalier de Bonvouloir* (Paris, 1953), p. 25. Guines to Vergennes, Sept. 8, 1775, AAE, CP, Angleterre, 511:369[vo].

[56] AAE, CP, Angleterre, 515:389–92

[57] See ibid., p. 14.

[58] AAE, MD, Etats-Unis, 1:105.

[59] AAE, CP, Angleterre, Supplement, 18:56; on the dating and significance of this document see John J. Meng, "A Footnote to Secret Aid in the American Revolution," *American Historical Review* 43 (1938): 791–95.

were capable of resisting the forces England had in America. But before they exhausted their limited resources, France had to help them.

The disappointing news of Washington's defeat at Long Island created some momentary doubts about the glowing reports of American military potential and the capacity of the Americans to continue the war.[60] But before the year 1776 ended Vergennes was minimizing the significance of the Long Island disaster.[61] Additional optimistic, indeed, exaggerated reports of American strength restored his confidence.[62] Later, the Battles of Saratoga and Germantown, as he perceived them at Versailles, further confirmed his opinion that the American army was strong, capable, and ready to launch an offensive war against the British.[63] Ironically, as Washington's shattered army settled down to the bitter winter at Valley Forge, Vergennes worried about the consequences that would follow if Washington captured Howe in Philadelphia. He feared that if the Americans won the war too quickly, they would owe France only a minimum of gratitude for their independence.[64]

After the signing of the Franco-American alliance, Conrad Alexandre Gérard, the first French minister to the United States, was assigned the task of reporting on the status of the American army. His first report was

[60] Doniol, *Histoire*, 1:615–16.

[61] See Vergennes, "Réflexions," Nov. 5, 1776, ibid., 1:680–82.

[62] See, for example, AAE, CP, Etats-Unis, 2:109, 110; Doniol, *Histoire*, 2:37; Deane to Vergennes, Mar. 22, 1777, AAE, CP, Etats-Unis, 2:141; Deane to Vergennes, May 12, 1777, ibid., p. 197.

[63] On the influence of Saratoga and Germantown on Vergennes's thinking, see the author's "The Battle of Germantown and the Franco-American Alliance of 1778," *Pennsylvania Magazine of History and Biography* 82 (1958): 55–64.

[64] See Doniol, *Histoire*, 2:623n.

a glowing one. The Continental army, he estimated, was 16,000 strong and on a very good footing. The militia was a body of soldiers characterized by courage and good will. Nearly every day, Gérard informed Vergennes, he saw the militia soldiers and recruits, and their appearance "did not deserve contempt." The Americans were so confident, he continued, that they were contemplating a campaign against the Indians of the Six Nations in western New York and were seriously considering a project for the invasion of Canada.[65]

Such an enthusiastic report was consistent with earlier but less reliable reports Vergennes had received from other sources; reports that confidently advanced the idea that the Americans were preparing for an early, vigorous campaign.[66] All the evidence seemed to support the French notion that if the Americans acted "with all their strength," they might defeat the army of General Howe. This appeared even more likely since they would soon be able to attack with the assurance of support by the comte d'Estaing's naval squadron.

A sentence in the instructions composed by Undersecretary Gérard de Rayneval for Gérard, but deleted by Vergennes in the final copy, demonstrates beyond question that Vergennes believed the American army capable of offensive operations. If d'Estaing's operations succeeded, the sentence stated, there would be nothing to keep the Americans from going on to conquer Nova Scotia and Canada while the French fleet swept the coasts of America and seized the islands

---

[65] Gérard to Vergennes, July 16, 1778, Meng, *Dispatches*, p. 158. For a more accurate estimate of the number of American soldiers at this moment, see Christopher Ward, *War of the Revolution*, 2 vols. (New York, 1952), 2:572.

[66] Arthur Lee to Vergennes, May 2, 1778, AAE, CP, Etats-Unis, 3:233–34.

around Newfoundland and Cape Breton.[67] The idea of conquering Nova Scotia and Canada was deleted, but not because Vergennes thought the Americans incapable of such an offensive. He feared they might succeed. He did not want Canada to become a fourteenth state of the United States.[68] He felt that if the future American nation had on its northern frontier a territory owned by a hostile power, it would be more apt to need the friendship of France.

Vergennes's image of the powerful American army could not survive. Gradually, Vergennes began to piece together another perception of American capabilities. It was an image of an army incapable of any major offensive action, an American Continental army and militia that were not reliable instruments of war, and, in fact, a military France could not safely count on. By October 1780 Lafayette was writing Washington that the "French Court have often complained to me of the inactivity of that American Army who before the alliance had distinguished themselves by their spirit of enterprise." French officials were of the opinion, Lafayette advised Washington, that the Americans, once the alliance was signed, had decided to let their ally fight their battles and were no longer willing to take any risks.[69]

There were, undoubtedly, those in America who would have been willing to let the French fight their battles; yet the new attitude of the French government was probably as much the result of earlier unrealistic appraisals of American strength as it was the consequence of deliberate inaction on the part of the Americans. Before the alliance Americans had created in

[67] Meng, *Dispatches,* p. 127.

[68] Vergennes to Gérard, Oct. 26, 1778, ibid., p. 359.

[69] Louis Gottschalk, ed., *Letters of Lafayette to Washington* (New York, 1944), p. 118.

France an image of a formidable American military potential. Furthermore, Washington's defensive, harassing, wearing-down strategy, so much praised before 1778, was not popular with Vergennes after the Franco-American alliance. Vergennes now expected a more active, offensive war from the citizen soldiers.

For a while after his arrival in America, Gérard himself believed that the American army was capable of taking the offensive. But the illusion did not last. His dispatches to Vergennes of August 1778, devoted entirely to the American army, indicate that Gérard was doing some intensive research.[70] He began his reappraisal with the fact that the size of the Continental army had been fixed by Congress at 44,000 men. But this quota, he told Vergennes, was far from being complete. The southern regiments were not even called up because their distance from the scene of operations made their transportation expensive and difficult. Even without the southern regiments Washington's army should have numbered 28,000 men. Yet there were hardly 15,000 in the army. Gérard drew some satisfaction from his research, however, because he learned that the English, too, were duped. They believed their enemy to be 30,000 strong.[71]

Furthermore, Gérard added, the spirit of liberty and the ambition to command, plus the vanity of titles and grades—"an epidemic sickness among the Americans" —made it difficult to enforce order and regularity in the military. It was Gérard's opinion that the people of America were too well off to take to soldiering.[72] In another dispatch he repeated the idea that the economic interests of Americans created difficulties for the mili-

[70] Gérard to Vergennes, Aug. 12, 1778, Meng, *Dispatches*, p. 209.

[71] Ibid., p. 214.

[72] Ibid., p. 215.

tary. Too many Americans wanted to profit from the war. "The spirit of mercentile cupidity," he said, "forms perhaps one of the most distinctive characteristics of the Americans and especially those people of the North and this characteristic will be an essential influence on the future destiny of the American Republic."[73]

The more information Vergennes received on the American army, the blacker the picture became. When he learned of the condition of the army at Valley Forge during the previous winter of 1777–78, it was black indeed. The army had lacked bread for entire days and in the middle of the forests soldiers had been without heat because their lack of shoes or stockings made it impossible to go and look for wood. "There were moments when this army had a strength of only five thousand men." It was astonishing that the English remained in Philadelphia during this time.[74]

As estimates of the insurgent army became more realistic, Vergennes's expectations for an American offensive diminished. After the British evacuated Philadelphia, the rumor began to circulate that New York was the next city from which they would withdraw, possibly going to the West Indies.[75] If the British were going to empty America of large units of their troops, perhaps they planned on changing the major theater of war. With British soldiers no longer an immediate threat, hopes for an American offensive would vanish.

The increasing difficulties of financing the army also made an offensive seem less likely. Vergennes learned that the money spent to maintain Washington's army of 15,000 men during the months of June, July, and August of 1778 would have supported an army of 60,000

[73] Ibid., p. 212.

[74] Gérard to Vergennes, Aug. 22, 1778, ibid., p. 232.

[75] Gérard to Vergennes, Sept. 10, 1778, ibid., p. 268–69.

men in Europe. Inflation was the key to this great difference. Merchandise was selling for from four to five times the prewar price. Recruiting, too, was subject to inflation. In September of 1778, to get a man to enlist for six months it was necessary to pay him up to five hundred dollars. The fighting spirit that the American people had first shown, Gérard informed Vergennes, had slackened so much that one could barely find recruits at that price.[76]

Furthermore, the opinion that the British were going to evacuate New York and possibly the continent appeared to have been sufficiently accepted in Congress to raise fears in France that the Americans were never going to go on the offensive. Fortunately, General Washington was not of this opinion and had let his ideas be known to Congress. Washington also urged Congress to take more vigorous measures to permit the army to carry on a more active campaign.[77] Nevertheless, Vergennes found no cause for encouragement in the intelligence reports. Gérard told him bluntly: "General cooling of all martial ardor among the people, the nonchalance with which some states furnish their military contingents, the miserly spirit could all lead to the Americans seizing the immediate advantages of a separate peace without considering the dangers involved nor of the long-range advantages to be drawn from a more enlightened policy." Gérard suggested to Vergennes that Congress might even desire a prolongation of the war if the main British efforts were turned against the French and the American continent were relatively free of British soldiers.[78]

Other sources told Vergennes the same thing. De

[76] Gérard to Vergennes, Sept. 15, 1778, ibid., p. 287.

[77] Gérard to Vergennes, Sept. 10, 1778, ibid., p. 279.

[78] Gérard to Vergennes, Sept. 20, 1778, ibid., pp. 301–2.

Kalb, who had gone to America with Lafayette, wrote him that a man accustomed to order and subordination continually suffered in the American army. One had to put up with many "irregularities" as well as a lack of discipline. Furthermore, de Kalb wrote, the officers and soldiers were characterized by a "crass ignorance" of the craft of war. At the same time, they all had a very high opinion of themselves. More serious still, de Kalb warned Vergennes, was the fact that the allies of the French were of English origin and it would be difficult to uproot their old hatred for France.[79] Lafayette too, began to doubt the sincerity of the American commitment. When questioned by a committee of Congress, he warned that Congress must not let all of the burden of the war fall on France.[80]

Did Vergennes believe these bleak evaluations of the American military? The evidence indicates that he did. He undoubtedly had some reservations about the accuracy of detail because he was acutely aware, from his own experience as a diplomat in the field, how difficult it was to gather and piece together such intelligence. Yet there is no question but that he grew increasingly anxious and discouraged with the performance of the American army. His disillusionment was no doubt partly the result of his earlier unrealistic views of the potential of the American military, but it followed, too, from his reading of the increasingly pessimistic reports of his agents. It was also a consequence of his conservative suspicions about the viability of republics. The American military lacked vigor, Vergennes believed, because the new United States was a republic governed by

[79] De Kalb to Vergennes, Sept. 7, 1778, AAE, CP, Etats-Unis, 5:28.

[80] Gérard to Vergennes, Oct. 20, 1778, Meng, *Dispatches*, pp. 339–40; Worthington C. Ford, ed., *Journals of the Continental Congress, 1774–1789*, 34 vols. (Washington, D.C., 1904–37), 12:1005.

a Congress unable by its very nature to provide strong leadership and support for its army. A few months after the signing of the Franco-American alliance, Vergennes declared to the French ambassador to Madrid that if the American republic did not correct its vices (and he considered it unlikely that it would do so), the American army would be forever weak and inactive. "I confess to you," he told Montmorin, "I have only a feeble confidence in the energy of the United States."[81] A few months later, he spoke of Congress's "habitual inertia" and pressed Gérard to do whatever he could to move it to do something to put the army in a state where it could take the offensive.[82] Congress, he had concluded, had its share of *"mauvaises tetes et coeurs peu honnetes"* ("hotheads and dishonest souls").[83] Whatever his pessimism about republics, the United States was nevertheless France's ally and the deteriorating American military perceived by Vergennes posed a critical problem for the French secretary of state. Repeatedly he urged the French representatives in America to press for more action on the part of the American military.[84]

But an offensive was beyond the means of the American forces. Vergennes recognized this when Gérard reported to him an interview between the French minister, the president of the Continental Congress, and General Washington. The conversation centered around what Gérard described as the "general state of the affairs of the Alliance" and on the necessity imposed by the treaty and the interests of the United States for an "active war" during the campaign of 1779. Gérard informed the Americans that France was not going to

[81] Vergennes to Montmorin, Nov. 27, 1778, Doniol, *Histoire,* 3:581.

[82] Vergennes to Gérard, July 18, 1779, ibid., 4:188.

[83] Vergennes to Montmorin, July 2, 1779, ibid., p. 239.

[84] Gérard to Vergennes, Oct. 20, 1778, Meng, *Dispatches,* p. 341.

demand efforts beyond their means but that everyone in France was expectant. A deliberate and voluntary inaction would make the United States appear wrong in the eyes of her allies.[85] When the president of the Continental Congress responded with reasons why the American army could not be more active, Gérard answered him by observing that Congress betrayed either its impotence or its unwillingness by not forcing the states to make more sacrifices in a cause that concerned liberty and independence.[86]

A few months later Vergennes received details of a report Washington had submitted to Congress concerning his army's potential. It contained hard evidence that the American army was in bad shape. Washington informed the Congress, Vergennes learned, that the fate of America might depend on one single setback. Washington found it impossible to hazard a decisive action with his army "which did not pass eight thousand men, neither disciplined, nor provisioned, having a great extent of land to guard against an experienced army provided in abundance with everything, and whose vessels offered an assured retreat." The American army even lacked the tools necessary to destroy the works at Stony Point after they had surprised and defeated their opponents there in July 1779.[87]

As Vergennes pondered these reports, Lafayette arrived in France to press the French for more aid to the insurgents. He asked for and received stands of arms and powder and other supplies to add to the additional three-million-livres loan that Franklin had already been able to get from Vergennes.[88] Moreover, in a letter to

[85] Gérard to Vergennes, Dec. 30, 1778, ibid., p. 456.

[86] Ibid., pp. 456–57.

[87] Gérard to Vergennes, July 31, 1779, ibid., p. 818.

[88] Louis Gottschalk, *Lafayette and the Close of the American Revolution* (Chicago, 1942), pp. 59–60.

Lafayette, Washington had hinted at the need for troops as well as supplies.[89] When Colonel de Fleury (another French officer recently returned from America) prepared a "Summary of the Political and Military State of America" for Lafayette, he also concluded that the Americans needed "clothes, arms, money, or, even still more, effective support."[90] Lafayette sent Colonel de Fleury to present this report to Vergennes.[91] Thus, while pro-American propaganda in France and at court had praised the high spirits of the American militia, the dogged determination of the Continental army, and the outstanding genius of George Washington, Vergennes came to perceive an army on the verge of disintegration and a Continental Congress unable to do anything about it. A French expeditionary force was required to support the crumbling American army, give it consistency, raise its morale, and spur it into action.[92]

In the spring of 1779 Anne César, chevalier de La Luzerne, replaced Gérard as the minister plenipotentiary to the United States. La Luzerne's reports added further evidence to Vergennes's bleak view of the American military.[93] Vergennes's recognition of the miserable plight of the American army led him to put even greater pressure on Congress to equip it for an offensive. Consequently, in January 1780 La Luzerne

[89] John C. Fitzpatrick, ed., *The Writings of George Washington from the Original Manuscripts, 1745–1799,* 39 vols. (Washington, D.C., 1931–44), 16:369–70.

[90] AAE, MD, Etats-Unis, 1:289–95; Gottschalk, *Lafayette and the Close of the American Revolution,* p. 61.

[91] Ibid., p. 61.

[92] Ibid., p. 63.

[93] John Durand, *New Materials for the History of the American Revolution* (New York, 1889), p. 217.

wrote to the president of the Continental Congress that he had received express orders to inform that assembly that another season of military campaigning was necessary. He went on to advise Congress that England was making preparations to continue the war "with vigor." France and Spain, La Luzerne said, would do their part to maintain control of the sea and to create a diversion in Europe and the West Indies. "It is absolutely necessary, [however], that the United States, on their part, should make efforts proportionable to the greatness of the object for which they are contending."[94]

La Luzerne also asked Congress "what force the United States can bring into the field [for the] next campaign; on what resources they rely for their maintenance and necessary appointments; and what shall be the general plan of campaign, on supposition either of having or not having the aid of ships of war." Congress replied "that the United States have expectations, on which they can rely with confidence, of bringing into the field an army of 25,000 effective men, exclusive of commissioned officers. That this army can be reinforced by militia, so as to be in force sufficient for any enterprise against the posts occupied by the enemy within the United States." With naval support, the answer went on, the United States could carry on an offensive war.[95]

If Vergennes was tempted to believe Congress's exaggerated expectations, he was soon set straight by a more honest measure of the American forces. From Morristown, New Jersey, Washington wrote to La Luzerne, who passed the information on to Versailles: "I with confidence assure your excellency that our force is

[94] Francis Wharton, ed., *Revolutionary Diplomatic Correspondence of the United States,* 6 vols. (Washington, D.C., 1889), 3:469.

[95] Ibid., p. 484.

so reduced by the expiration of the terms for which a considerable part of it was engaged and will be so much more diminished in the course of a month or two from the same cause, as scarcely to suffice for the exigence of the service, and to afford just cause for uneasiness should the enemy be actuated by a spirit of enterprise before we receive the reinforcements intended for the next campaign."[96] The 25,000-man army promised by Congress was, apparently, to be built from almost nothing. Washington had precious little of it under his command. In fact, Congress's army existed only on paper. Clearly there were some Americans who wanted to hide the miserable state of American affairs from the French.

That Vergennes recognized the gravity of the problem is demonstrated by his repeated decisions, at great cost to France, to provide the American soldiers with the necessities to carry on the war. In June 1780, convinced by Franklin of the dire straits of the American army, he arranged an advance on a loan to permit Franklin to purchase uniforms for 10,000 soldiers.[97] At the same time he impressed upon Lafayette, who was returning to the United States, that the Americans had to make a much greater effort in the war if they really wanted to establish their independence.[98]

Disturbed by the reports of the American army's poverty, Vergennes had even ordered his ambassador in Madrid to approach the Spanish to see if they would supply some of the needs of the American soldiers who, he told Montmorin, required "everything: money, uniforms, shoes, artillery, arms and munitions." He had a long list of things the Americans urgently needed, he

[96] Ibid., p. 498.

[97] Doniol, *Histoire*, 4:285.

[98] Vergennes to Lafayette, June 3, 1780, ibid., p. 350.

said, and he could see no way France could furnish them all.[99]

Meanwhile, Vergennes had La Luzerne keep the pressure on Congress. The French envoy's method was to prick them with their own exaggerated promises. He reminded the president of the Continental Congress that "the King after the positive assurances which he has received has not the least doubt that *the American army is now twenty-five thousand strong, not including commissioned officers, and that it is at this moment in a condition to undertake the most vigorous offensive operations against the enemy in the posts which he occupies within the territory of the United States.*" La Luzerne himself underlined for emphasis his repetition of the words that Congress had used in its response to his question as to the probable strength of the Revolutionary army for the campaign of the summer of 1780. The lash was cruel, but conditions demanded it. When the French generals arrived, they expected to find "forces respectable in numbers ready to enter upon action."[100]

Yet it is doubtful that Vergennes now expected the American army to be on an effective footing of 25,000 men. In April 1780 La Luzerne had informed him that the weakness of the American army in the winter of 1779–80 had been such as to prevent Washington from going to Philadelphia to see the French minister.[101] Soon after his arrival in the United States, General Rochambeau informed Versailles that Washington had only 3,000 men under his orders. "Send us troops, vessels and money," he urged, "but don't count on these people here nor on their means."[102] La Luzerne agreed.

---

[99] Vergennes to Montmorin, Apr. 12, 1779, ibid., 3:753.

[100] Wharton, *Revolutionary Diplomatic Correspondence*, 3:804.

[101] Doniol, *Histoire*, 4:349.

[102] Ibid., 5:344–45.

"I was afraid," he wrote Vergennes, "that there was a concerted plan to exaggerate the suffering of the army, but on my way through camp [La Luzerne had just visited Washington's camp at Morristown, N.J.] I myself saw the constant recurrence of its necessities, the Generals being often unable to show themselves to the men without demands made upon them for bread and clothes."[103] Not long after this letter was written the Pennsylvania and New Jersey lines revolted against their miserable conditions.

Vergennes was deeply worried. The American army seemed on the verge of collapse and unable to act, while the Continental Congress manufactured paper armies of 25,000 men. At the same time the costs of maintaining the American army soared and France was asked to pay. "Congress relies too heavily on France for subsidies to maintain their army," Vergennes complained.[104] Meanwhile, not long after he had read the reports on Rochambeau's meeting with Washington at Hartford in September 1780 and the news of the revolt of the Pennsylvania and New Jersey soldiers, Vergennes confronted the likelihood that the American military might dissolve altogether. If the spirit of revolt continued and the American army disintegrated, he advised La Luzerne, the French army should remain in Rhode Island and prepare to withdraw from the continent.[105] Vergennes now saw that the American army was in "extreme distress."[106] The military implications for France's expeditionary force in America had been made

[103] Durand, *New Materials,* p. 221.

[104] Waldo G. Leland and Edmund C. Burnett, eds., "Letters from Lafayette to Luzerne, 1780–1782," *American Historical Review* 20 (1915): 582–83.

[105] Vergennes to La Luzerne, Mar. 9, 1781, Doniol, *Histoire,* 4:585.

[106] Vergennes to La Luzerne, Apr. 19, 1781, ibid., p. 589.

clear to Rochambeau. The secretary of state for war ordered him, "If the American army comes to the point of dissolving," to refuse all requests to penetrate into the continent and to await the king's orders to retire to the Antilles or Santo Domingo.[107] When the news of the victory at Yorktown arrived at Versailles, it must have appeared to Vergennes as the later American peace treaty with England appeared to Rayneval: a "miracle,"[108] but a miracle made possible only because of the presence of the French army under Rochambeau.

If Vergennes perceived the American military to be so unreliable, why did he continually urge that it become more active? We can only speculate, but it seems likely that his deep-seated distrust of all forms of parliamentary government led him to believe that the Continental Congress did not create a viable conventional army because it did not try hard enough to do so. Hence the repeated pressuring and badgering of Congress to do more. Also, Vergennes's incessant urging for more activity on the part of the Americans was undoubtedly the result of his growing awareness that France's resources were limited and France was rapidly approaching those limits. The Americans, he clearly believed, had become too dependent on France. And, finally, it is probable that Vergennes did not really understand what the American army was, in fact, doing. The irregular, guerrilla-type war fought by many of the American soldiers and militia was largely beyond the appreciation of most Europeans familiar with conventional warfare. In light of Vergennes's perceptions of the Americans, John Adams's repeated pronouncements that Americans would be dependent on no one must have seemed like empty rhetoric if not downright

[107] Ibid., p. 549.

[108] Rayneval to Vergennes, Jan. 28, 1783, ibid., 5:286.

insanity. The young, weak United States was, in Vergennes's view, by no means independent.

When the peace treaties were finally signed in 1783 and the war ended, Vergennes felt obliged to summarize for Louis XVI the results of almost five years of war and diplomacy.[109] It is difficult to gauge just how much he believed his justification of past decisions. During the peace negotiations he was under severe pressure and criticism from various factions in the French government and court because he refused to continue the war in order to gain more territory and colonies for France, especially in India.[110] In the King's council the duc de Castries repeatedly resisted Vergennes's policies which, he felt, left France to carry all the burdens of the war while her allies made off with the rewards.[111] If Vergennes had any reservations or disappointments about his past diplomacy, he was not inclined to articulate them; his enemies could use his words against him. His perceptions of the results of his diplomacy are, therefore, as much briefs for the defense as they are objective analyses.

Nevertheless, his comments about the war contain several recurring ideas worth noting. It is clear, for example, that he did not regret having brought France into the war despite the government's near-bankrupt treasury. In March 1784 he argued that England's pride, ambition, violence, and injustices had provoked Louis XVI to intervening in order to prevent the Amer-

[109] Mémoire présenté au Roi par le Comte de Vergennes Mar. 29, 1784, AAE, MD, France, 587: 207–25.

[110] See Dupont to Vergennes, Jan. 4, 1782, de Lessait to Vergennes, June 12, 1782, and La Toul to Vergennes, Aug. 29, 1782, AAE, CP, Angleterre, 536:13 ff., 537:234 ff., and 285 ff.

[111] René de la Croix, duc de Castries, Le Testament de La Monarchie (Paris, 1958–59), pp. 259–61.

ican Revolutionary War from developing into something "prejudicial" to France.[112] The intervention was just one among several examples, according to Vergennes, of the king's desire to preserve public order and to act as the arbiter. France had no need for aggrandizement or conquests, but as the arbiter of Europe she was concerned with maintaining the balance of power.

In addition, Vergennes claimed that, as a result of France's moderation during the war, the small powers no longer feared France's ambitions. Even the Dutch, he pointed out, after more than a century of suspicions of France, had broken with their long-standing ally, England, and fought with France during the war.[113] This about-face, Vergennes believed, was a major victory for France.

Vergennes admitted that the progress of the war had not always developed according to plan and that there had been mistakes committed and reverses suffered. But he reminded his monarch that the primary aim of the war—American independence—had been, in fact, achieved.[114]

Vergennes also felt that the war justified the government's earlier decision to give top priority to the expansion of the French navy. While he vaguely recognized that orderly finances and a well-constituted army were important, he insisted that a well-organized and carefully maintained navy should always have first priority. "I humbly plead with you," he urged Louis XVI, "to keep the navy on a respectable footing."[115] Power, he

---

[112] Mémoire présenté au Roi par le Comte de Vergennes, Mar. 29, 1784, AAE, MD, France, 587:207.

[113] Ibid., pp. 210–11.

[114] Ibid., pp. 211–11vo.

[115] Ibid., pp. 223vo–24.

told the king, was still the most certain way to gain respect, especially if the power was used wisely and for justice.[116]

The peace treaty signed with England made provision for negotiating an Anglo-French commercial treaty that Vergennes hoped could begin a rapprochement between England and France. He continued to press for the treaty until it was signed in 1786. Yet despite his official stance in 1784, Vergennes in his postwar communications with Louis XVI continued to see Great Britain as France's first enemy. This "proud and haughty" nation, he warned Louis, would reopen a war with France again whenever she believed herself able to win it. In fact, Vergennes concluded, England was already busily building the ships to fight that next war.[117]

Thus, the war did nothing to change Vergennes's mind about war: it was inevitable, and France must forever spend her resources preparing for it. One should not "flatter oneself" with the idea of a long peace, he declared. The newly won peace, he believed, was "absolutely precarious."[118]

Nor, apparently, did Vergennes learn much during the war about France's growing inability to continue using its resources to fight wars. He had, of course, recognized that France needed to put her finances in order to avoid bankruptcy, but it was England, not France, according to his perceptions, which had really exhausted itself during the war. And it was England, he informed Louis XVI in 1784, just three years before France went bankrupt from the debts of the American

[116] Ibid., p. 223vo.

[117] Ibid., p. 224.

[118] Ibid., p. 224vo; see also Vergennes to Louis XVI, Mar. 29, 1784, A.N., K164:3.

war, which emerged from the war "bent under the weight of an enormous debt which was crushing her."[119]

[119] Mémoire présenté au Roi par le Comte de Vergennes, Mar. 29, 1784, AAE, MD, France, 587:207.

LAWRENCE S. KAPLAN

The Treaties of Paris and Washington, 1778 and 1949

Reflections on Entangling Alliances

THERE IS A special source of inspiration for this essay that links the treaties of alliance of 1778 and 1949 with the Capitol Historical Society proceedings of 1978. Senate Caucus Room 318, where the four major contributors to this conference made their presentations, was also the place where Cornell professor Curtis P. Nettels spoke at great length and with much passion on May 17, 1949, on reasons why the Senate Foreign Relations Committee should reject the newly signed North Atlantic Treaty. The pact, according to Nettels, was an entangling alliance that would produce unhappy consequences. By joining the Atlantic alliance the United States would "abandon the historic policies of the Nation and substitute therefor a new policy utterly alien to our traditions. We are asked to forsake the unbroken practice of 149 years—the practice of abstaining from peacetime military alliances. We are asked to reject the wisest counsel of the farewell address—that which warns against habitual favoritism and habitual animosity toward particular nations."[1]

There was nothing elliptical about Nettels's warning. The year 1949 marked the 149th, as he noted, since the United States had formally terminated its one entangling alliance with a European power. The Convention of 1800 ending the Quasi War with France had disengaged the United States from an association that had confirmed the worst American suspicions about the evils of Europe: namely, that a small, innocent, and virtuous people would be betrayed by a large exploitive ally. George Washington had explained in his Farewell Address that "an attachment of a small and weak toward a great and powerful nation dooms the former to be the satellite of the latter."[2] It did not seem to occur to Nettels that the "great and powerful nation" in 1949 was the United States when he equated the secret Franco-Spanish intrigue of 1779 with the Anglo-Russian Treaty of 1942 or the Franco-Russian Treaty of 1944. Nothing had changed in his view. If Washington had been alive in 1949, he would have repeated his Farewell Address of 1796.

Nettels touched on an enduring theme in American history, the force of isolationism as a protective shield against the wiles of the Old World. The word *alliance* conjured up for him and for many others all the damage that a political connection with Europe had done to the United States in the past and presumably could do in the future.

The differences between the image and the reality of alliance merit more examination than they usually receive. Does an alliance necessarily entangle? If so, does

[1] "North Atlantic Treaty," *Hearings,* U.S. Committee on Foreign Relations, 81st Cong. 1st sess., 3 vols. (Washington, D.C., 1949), 3:1121.

[2] James D. Richardson, ed., *A Compilation of the Messages and Papers of the Presidents, 1789–1897,* 10 vols. (Washington, D.C. 1889), 1:222.

the entanglement necessarily benefit the large partner at the expense of the small? If the advantages are mutual, can they be weighed? In light of these questions I wish to examine both the Paris treaties of 1778 and the Treaty of Washington of 1949. I propose to link 1778, when anxious Americans went for help to Paris in their war against Great Britain, with 1949, when anxious Europeans assembled in Washington to seek American support for their efforts to contain Communist power.

However tainted the idea of alliance may be to the American mind, it has been a fact of world affairs for millenia and a central fact of the nation-state system since the Renaissance. While idealistic purposes may be proclaimed as the objective of the alliance, as in the support of neutral rights in the treaty of amity and commerce of 1778 or as in the encouragement of an Atlantic community in the North Atlantic Treaty, these are usually either minor notes or hypocritical ones to mask immediate and practical bargains. A quid is given for a quo; benefits are measured against drawbacks. And they are often psychological in nature. Deterrence against an enemy attack is frequently identified as the most vital function of the North Atlantic Treaty, with the end product being a more satisfactory state of Western Europe's sense of security. Such is the general nature of a defensive alliance. The Franco-American alliance, on the other hand, was a classic example of an offensive alliance, designed to increase the power of one side to combat more effectively an opposing side.

In both instances the allying process by the larger ally was intended to redress a faltering balance of power. George Liska has made the point that "alliances are against, and only derivatively for, someone or something."[3] Their intention, as in the case of the North

---

[3] George Liska, *Nations in Alliance: The Limits of Independence* (Baltimore, 1968), p. 13.

Atlantic Treaty, may be to relieve allies from pressures exerted against them by another power. The United States as the core power was the vital ingredient in this process of deterrence in 1949. Only later, after the outbreak of war in Korea, did deterrence appear to require military organization to continue functioning effectively. The purpose of the alliance with France in 1778, on the other hand, was to coerce Britain into accepting the complete independence of the United States. The French decision for alliance was also a decision for war. The British required, in the French view, a reduction of the pride and power which they had gained from the Seven Years' War, and the American rebellion would be the instrument for Vergennes to achieve this goal.

The costs of alliance have to be measured carefully by stronger and weaker ally alike. The latter naturally worries about the potential neglect of its vital interests as the larger power pursues larger objectives through the alliance. The former in turn must be concerned about overextending its resources through its commitment as well as sacrificing its freedom of action to a smaller, possibly irresponsible, ally that might take actions binding the larger without fear of their consequences.

All these considerations were present in 1778. The Founding Fathers looked carefully at the possibilities inherent in French reactions to the American Revolution. John Adams asked all the right questions in March 1776:

> How is the Interest of France and Spain affected by the dispute between B. and the C[olonies]? Is it the Interest of France [to] stand neuter, to join with B. or to join with the C? Is it not in her Interest, to dismember the B. Empire? Will her Dominions be safe, if B. and A[merica] remain connected? Can she preserve her possessions in the W. I.? She has in the W. I.

> Martinico, Guadeloupe, and one half of Hispaniola.
> In Case a Reconciliation should take Place, between
> B. and A. and a War should break out between B.
> and France, would not all her Islands be taken from
> her in 6 Months? [4]

Similarly, at this time and later, French ministers spec-
ulated on the advantages and disadvantages of supporting the colonists. Drains on the treasury, dangerous
comfort to republicanism, and loss of opportunity to
acquire Austrian Flanders were balanced against considerations of reducing British power and arrogance,
restoring lost territories in the New World, and replac-
ing Britain as the beneficiary of American commerce. [5]
What is missing in these rational considerations are
the irrational, the illogical, the emotional elements that
intrude to push policymakers into actions against their
own interests or to raise expectations that could never
be fulfilled. In the course of American colonial history
there had developed an isolationist attitude toward the
Old World that distorted as it informed the American
understanding of an alliance with France. American isolationism gave a perspective to the Franco-American
connection which not only led inevitably to the conclusion that the large ally manipulated the small but that a
large European power would always damage Americans
in any entangling relationship.

The United States was heir to an isolationist tradition
that found a moral distinction separating Americans
from Europeans. Europe represented tyranny, poverty,
and superstition while America was home to freedom,

[4] Lyman Butterfield et al., eds., *Diary and Autobiography of John
Adams,* Mar. 1, 1776, 4 vols. (Cambridge, Mass., 1961), 2:235.

[5] Samuel Flagg Bemis, *The Diplomacy of the American Revolution*
(New York, 1935), pp. 70 ff.

opportunity, and tolerance. Politically, it meant a republic as opposed to a monarchy; socially, it implied fluid class lines as opposed to the rigidity of a European caste system; religiously, it signified the triumph of free expression as opposed to European establishments; and economically, it presented a contrast between a land available to all who wanted it and a continent where too little land supported too many people.

Responding to these distinctions at the time of the American Revolution, Hector St. John de Crèvecoeur called the American "this new man."[6] It did not matter that American self-perceptions may not have been warranted by the historical evidence; it mattered that those who made the Revolution shared these perceptions and promulgated them with all their distortions in the Declaration of Independence. That document minimized the British origins of the colonies and maximized the differences between Europeans and Americans, between two different peoples who would separate because one of them had broken the contract that had earlier connected them.

Absurd as this interpretation of the British Empire may have been to Englishmen, it had been nourished by more than a century of experience during which time the colonies managed their own affairs with little British interference. Britain came to be considered a distant patron, a sometimes uncertain ally against the Spanish, French, or Indians, a business partner who took advantage of virtuous Americans, a corrupt feudal superior who not only exploited Americans but implicated them in its alien dynastic interests. The Declaration dissolved an undesirable political connection with that nation and presented the thirteen United States to "a candid world" as a species of a new and better order of humanity.

[6] Hector St. John de Crèvecoeur, *Letters from an American Farmer* (1782) (New York, 1957), p. 39.

Analysts such as Felix Gilbert have found in this American sense of superiority a wish to serve the world by creating in its own experiment a way of achieving a better society for all peoples. Such is the message he has read in the Model Treaty of 1776, in which the new nation appeared to seek aid abroad to advance an idealistic foreign policy. The avoidance of political entanglement and the support of free trade in the treaty plan may be seen, then, as a means of breaking down all artificial barriers to peace as well as eliminating the props of war. Gilbert found isolationism to have been in the service of an international idea, and "the logical consequence was that in a reformed world, based on reason, foreign policy and diplomacy would become unnecessary, that the new world would be a world without diplomats."[7]

But the Model Treaty, as James H. Hutson has recently pointed out, essentially "proposed commercial reciprocity rather than commercial freedom."[8] Americans wanted from nonentanglement neither an absolute isolation from the outside world nor an international Utopia, but rather their opportunity to manipulate the resources of the New World desired by the Old to win their independence. Foreign relations from the beginning were designed to help the new nation through a difficult birth. Thomas Paine pointed the way in *Common Sense* when he wrote that "the true interest of America is to steer clear of Europe's contentions, which she never can do while, by her dependence on Britain, she is made the makeweight in the scale of British politics." At the same time Paine saw that American commerce, if "well attended to, will secure us the peace and

[7] Felix Gilbert, *To the Farewell Address: Ideas of Early American Foreign Policy* (Princeton, 1961), p. 66.

[8] James H. Hutson, "Early American Diplomacy: A Reappraisal," in Lawrence S. Kaplan, ed., *The American Revolution and "A Candid World"* (Kent, Ohio, 1977), p. 45.

friendship of all Europe." Hence, the many disadvantages of being connected to Britain, and "our duty to mankind at large, as well as to ourselves," should lead Americans "to renounce the alliance; because any submission to, or dependence on, Great Britain, tends directly to involve this continent in European wars and quarrels, and set us at variance with nations who would otherwise seek our friendship, and against whom we have neither anger nor complaint. As Europe is our market for trade, we ought to form no partial connection with any part of it."[9]

There has been no better definition of American isolationism than in *Common Sense.* Paine did not call for a policy that would change the balance-of-power system as many philosophers of the day had wanted. He urged Americans to exploit Europe's need for American products, an idea that obviously impressed John Adams when he recommended to his colleagues on the committee preparing the Model Treaty "that we should avoid all Alliance, which might embarrass Us in after times and might involve us in future European Wars. That a Treaty of commerce which would opperate [*sic*] as a Repeal of the British Acts of Navigation as far as respected Us and Admit France into an equal participation of the benefits of our commerce . . . would be an ample Compensation to France for Acknowledging our Independence."[10]

The language of the treaty plan contained the same confident tones. The terms for the most part dealt with the many commercial benefits for the two countries that would come from "a firm, inviolable, and universal peace, and a true and sincere friendship between the

[9] Thomas Paine, *Common Sense,* in Moncure D. Conway, ed., *The Writings of Thomas Paine,* 4 vols. (New York, 1967), 1:88–89.

[10] Butterfield, *Adams Diary and Autobiography,* 3:337–38.

most serene and mighty prince, Lewis the sixteenth . . . and the US."[11] With a show of generosity Article XII of the model would allow the French to retain their access to American fisheries which they had received in 1763. But the king of France was admonished in Article IX never "under any pretence" to attempt to take any part of Canada or Florida or any other part of North America, since it was understood that the United States would take over all territories on the continent that had been under British rule. While there was no specific instruction to the French to enter the war, it certainly was expected. Should Britain declare war against the French in consequence of French aid to the United States, the Americans graciously promised under Article VIII not to assist the British in this circumstance.[12]

What could justify the arrogance of a small, untried republic, lacking a treasury and an army, in offering such an agreement to France? The answer must lie in Paine's and Adams's premise that America was a prize for which Europe should compete, that Britain's folly in abusing the mainspring of its preeminence as a world power should be invitation enough to win France's full assistance without a significant cost to the United States. They were mistaken. When they discovered that their self-confidence was misplaced, the suspicions about all Europeans deepened. The difficulty the Americans subsequently experienced in convincing the French to join their cause served ultimately to convince them that entanglement was dangerous.

But in the short run the Continental Congress did not have the luxury of choice. Its bargaining power declined with Washington's military fortunes in 1776 and

---

[11] "Plan of a Treaty with France," *Secret Journals of the Congress of the Confederation*, 4 vols. (Boston, 1821), 2:7.

[12] Ibid., p. 11.

1777, with a consequent softening of the terms the United States would accept for French aid. The congressional commissioners Benjamin Franklin, Silas Deane, and Arthur Lee were instructed as they left for their assignment in Paris to forego demanding from the French the same freedom of commerce that the United States would grant to France, "rather than obstruct the farther progress of the treaty."[13] By the end of 1776 Congress was even prepared to meet almost any objection France or any other potential ally might have just to win their immediate approval. A note of desperation can be found in the communications from the Committee of Secret Correspondence to their commissioners abroad.[14]

When France continued to hesitate in the face of the projected costs of the war and the uncertainty of American fortunes, the commissioners tried mixing blandishments with threats. The French were reminded that Britain's present superiority rested on its control of the American continent and that if the French cooperated with the Americans the power that had been Britain's would then be France's.[15] Additionally, the British West Indies were held out as a reward for entry into the war.[16] A failure to act could mean the subjugation of Americans who might be persuaded by the British into

[13] In Appendix IV (a), in Richard Henry Lee, *Life of Arthur Lee*, 2 vols. (Boston, 1829), 1:280.

[14] B. Harrison et al., Committee of Secret Correspondence, to the Commissioners at Paris, Dec. 30, 1776, in Francis Wharton, ed., *Revolutionary Diplomatic Correspondence of the United States*, 6 vols. (Washington, D.C., 1889), 2:240.

[15] Committee on Foreign Affairs to Commissioners in France, May 30, 1777, Papers of the Continental Congress, Reel 105, Library of Congress.

[16] Jan. 5, 1777, Franklin, Deane, and Lee to Vergennes, Wharton, *Revolutionary Diplomatic Correspondence*, 2:246.

joining them to help make Britain conquerors of the world.[17]

As time went by the quiet hints became open pleadings, asking France to divert British forces in 1777 before they destroyed the Revolution. If America fell, Deane warned, all Europe would suffer from British arrogance; Lee commented bitterly that "we are left, like Hercules in his cradle, to strangle the serpent that annoys all Europe."[18] Finally, they observed that if France did not seize its opportunity to help itself as well as to help the former colonies, the Americans would have no choice but to reunite with Britain, which would endanger French interests everywhere. "The power of Great Britain and N. America divided can never be so dangerous to her," Richard Henry Lee observed, "as when united, abstracted from the consideration of gratitude that must bind her to the affection of our virtuous young republic for timely and effectual aid afforded them in the day of their distress."[19] With greater subtlety and appreciation for French sensibilities Benjamin Franklin pursued the same course of cajoling, intimidating, flattering, and promising the potential ally a variety of benefits if it should respond and warning of dire consequences if it should turn away from the United States.

When the great day arrived and France finally responded with two treaties in February 1778, the initial American reaction was one of enormous relief and gratitude. There was no upbraiding the commissioners for abandoning the Model Treaty of 1776, nor was there

[17] June 7, 1777, Deane to Dumas, Wharton, *Revolutionary Diplomatic Correspondence*, 2:332–33.

[18] Arthur Lee to Baron Schulenberg, June 10, 1777, 2:334.

[19] Richard Henry Lee to Arthur Lee, Apr. 20, 1777, Lee Family Papers, Reel 3, Library of Congress.

any regret expressed in the Congress for the abandonment of the ideal of nonentanglement. Instead, the hard-pressed Congress was anxious "to present the grateful acknowledgments . . . to his Most Christian Majesty for his truly magnanimous conduct respecting these States in the said generous and disinterested treaties."[20] They spoke for the nation at this moment, and the warm rush of good feeling for France was to be expressed periodically over the next generation.

Yet the reactions of gratitude and relief were superficial and transitory. The reality of 1778 was that the treaty of alliance, if not the treaty of amity and commerce, represented a sharp retreat from the bright promise of 1776. It was clearly an entangling alliance, made at the behest of the superior power. As Article VIII explicitly noted, "Neither of the two Parties shall conclude either Truce or Peace with Great Britain, without the formal consent of the other first obtain'd." In other words, the Americans could make no separate arrangement with Great Britain, could not terminate the war unilaterally, even if its objectives had been won, without the approval of an ally whose terms for ending the conflict might not be in consonance with American interests. This was the essence of entanglement. The relationship was further complicated by Article XI, wherein the United States was required to guarantee "from the present time and forever, against all other powers, to wit, the United States to his Most Christian Majesty, the present Possessions of the Crown of France in America as well as those which it may acquire by the future Treaty of peace."[21] This article bound the

[20] May 4, 1778, Wharton, *Revolutionary Diplomatic Correspondence*, 2:569.

[21] David Hunter Miller, *Treaties and Other International Acts of the United States of America*, 8 vols. (Washington, D.C., 1931), 2:568–69.

United States to the defense of the French West Indies in the event of a future war as well as during the present Anglo-French conflict.

So rather than confirm American belief in their ability to manipulate European powers, the anxieties suffered by the Congress in Philadelphia and by its commissioners in Paris over French hesitations confirmed their belief in the unreliability of the Old World and narrowed the distinctions between the past evils of their former imperial masters and the potential threats of other European nations. France was perceived to have entered the war grudgingly, for its own advantage, and at the moment of its own choosing. It exacted a price the Americans had no wish to pay, including the exercise of proconsular powers by the French ministers in Philadelphia from 1779 to 1782.[22] The great power had its own ulterior motives and a world scheme that could severely limit the freedom of action of the small power. If France gave its blessing to the principle of freedom of the seas, this was not a blow on behalf of morality or a conversion to a new view of international relations; it was a short-term ploy in a long-term opposition to the maritime strength of England. Once the euphoria over France's action had passed, the United States was left with all its suspicions of Europe intact.

The sluggishness of France's military and naval activity in America over the next few years served to reinforce doubts. But this problem was remediable, as the triumph of Yorktown showed. More difficult to exorcise was the renunciation of the right to make peace with Britain on their own and the knowledge that the United States was obligated to come to the aid of France in the West Indies whenever the French should ask. The latter

[22] William C. Stinchcombe, *The American Revolution and the French Alliance* (Syracuse, N.Y. 1969), pp. 68–69, 122–23, 132, and 157–62.

issue would distress American diplomats for a generation. The former raised immediate difficulties. While John Jay was in Spain in 1779 seeking vainly for formal recognition of the United States, France had made a secret arrangement to bring Spain into the war with the restoration of Gibraltar as the prize. Without its knowledge the United States was obligated to continue fighting until France had wrested Gibraltar from Britain, an objective Britain would contest more fiercely than any in North America and one in which America had no national interest.[23] This was the acting out of entanglement.

Worse was yet to come. In 1782, as the war appeared stalemated after the Battle of Yorktown, John Jay discovered that Gérard de Rayneval, undersecretary of France's foreign secretary, Charles Gravier, comte de Vergennes, had met secretly in London with Spanish and British representatives to consider terms for ending the war.[24] While they spoke of independence for the United States, they also proposed to concede to the British the boundaries of the Quebec Act, the territory from the Great Lakes to the Ohio River. The area south of the Ohio would be set aside for an Indian buffer state under Spanish protection. The result would be the confinement of the new nation to the Atlantic coastal strip and the denial to Americans of the lands west of the Appalachians. When this information reached Jay and John Adams, they eventually convinced a more trusting Franklin that France was prepared to sell out America to appease the more important ally, Spain. If Spain could not win Gibraltar—and after French naval defeat in the Caribbean in 1782, the prospect was most un-

[23] See Richard B. Morris, *The Peacemakers: The Great Powers and American Independence* (New York, 1965), pp. 15–17.

[24] Ibid., pp. 328–32.

likely—the Spanish could at least gain security in North America against the westward pressures of the former colonists.

Word of these negotiations guided American behavior in the separate agreement with Britain. Rightly or wrongly, the perception of betrayal, or potential betrayal, encouraged the most pessimistic conclusions to be drawn from French activities with respect to the peace treaty. If a sinister interpretation could be given to any particular French position, the commissioners were prepared to accept it. Difficulties over American claims to a share in the fisheries off the shores of Canada became part of a French plot to sabotage American interests in collaboration with the British enemy. Similarly, Vergennes's insistence upon some American compensation to loyalists for their loss of property was construed, particularly by John Adams, as an act of hostility. "What can be their Motives," he asked rhetorically, "to become the Advocates of the Tories?" And he had the answer. It would be to make more difficult any understanding between the United States and Great Britain.[25] For others, like John Mercer, a Virginia delegate to the Continental Congress, the mysterious meetings in London presaged a coalition of British and French against Americans.[26] Moved by these considerations and others, Franklin and his colleagues may have had qualms about the consequences but no doubts about the rightness of their decision to make peace on their own with Britain in defiance of their formal instructions from the Congress.

Despite these suspicions of France, the signing of

[25] Butterfield, *Adams Diary and Autobiography*, Nov. 11, 1782, 3:52.

[26] Notes on Debates in the Congress of the Confederation, Mar. 19, 1783, in William C. Hutchinson et al., eds., *The Papers of James Madison*, 12 vols. to date (Chicago and Charlottesville, Va., 1962-), 6:358–59.

peace terms with Britain did not signal an American intention to undo the alliance. Even such a Francophobe as John Jay recognized and appreciated the continuing American need for French financial help. While he was sure that the French "are not a moral people," as he assured Adams in the heat of the conflict of 1782, he told Robert Livingston, the secretary for foreign relations in Philadelphia, "Let us be honest and grateful to France, but let us think for ourselves."[27]

When Americans thought for themselves and acted on their own behalf, they would see that the French, even the most benevolent of them, wished to keep the Americans under their control. A weak and divided America would serve their purpose, as many in the Congress understood. Hamilton, for example, felt it "not improbable that it had been the policy of France to procrastinate the definite acknowledgment of our Independence on the part of GB in order to keep us more knit to herself & untill her own interests could be negotiated."[28]

As this wave of skepticism engulfed the counsels of the Congress and the commissioners, it was not accompanied by any concomitant appreciation for Great Britain. There was no doubt about the intentions of its negotiator, Richard Oswald, to divide Americans from their French ally. Adams informed Oswald that if Britain would treat America as genuinely independent of the former mother country, there would be no alliance with France. "Take care to remove from the American Mind all Cause of Fear of You. No other Motive but Fear of You will ever produce in the Americans an unreasonable Attachment to the house of Bourbon." But,

[27] Butterfield, *Adams Diary and Autobiography,* Nov. 5, 1782, 3:46–47. Jay to Livingston, Sept. 18, 1782, John Jay Papers, Library of Congress.

[28] Harold C. Syrett, ed., *The Papers of Alexander Hamilton,* 26 vols. to date (New York, 1961–), 3:294–95.

he pointed out, "if you pursue the Plan of cramping, clipping and weakening America, on the Supposition that She will be a Rival to you, you will make her really so, you will make her the natural and perpetual Ally of your natural and perpetual Ennemies."[29] This was wasted effort, and Adams knew it. The British had learned nothing, he noted, and he expected nothing from them.

Even those congressmen in Philadelphia who believed that the commissioners should have shown more consideration for their ally had little faith in the good intentions of France. Some worried that Jay or Adams had been "ensnared by the dexterity of the British Minister."[30] But sentiments that sounded more Francophilic than Anglophobic did not necessarily reveal any sense of fraternity with the French. Fear lay behind them. When John Mercer spoke of censuring the commissioners for violating their instructions and for behaving in manner "expressive of their distrust" of France, he did not deny reasons for distrust, only their expression. Retribution, not guilt, dishonor, or ingratitude, was his concern because France, "in case of our basely disappointing her, may league with our Enemy for our destruction and for a division of the spoils."[31] The Confederation Congress was well aware of the response of Marbois, the chargé d'affaires in Philadelphia, that "great powers never *complained*, but that they *felt & remembered*."[32] The price of the French alliance could be burdensome.

At the same time, the United States continued to be dependent on the relationship for further loans, a prob-

[29] Butterfield, *Adams Diary and Autobiography*, Dec. 9, 1782, 3:91.

[30] Notes on Debates, March 12–15, 1783, Hutchinson, *Madison Papers*, 6:328.

[31] Ibid., Mar. 19, 1783, 6:358.

[32] Ibid., Mar. 15, 1783, 6:329.

lem that raised another facet of entanglement in the Congress. While the need for funds was desperate, should they be solicited if their known purpose was to bind Americans all the more firmly to what all recognized to be a dangerous connection? Robert Morris, the superintendent of finance, promised that "it will be my constant study to draw from our own resources and less on our demands on France but these things require time." If there should be no alternative, he would prefer a loan rather than a gift in order to lessen the weight of the obligation to France.[33] Given Morris's extensive private business dealings with the Ancien Régime, his cautionary note may have reflected reasons other than the national interest; but even so they tell a story of the balance between entanglement and independence. By the end of the war the alliance of 1778 was no longer important to the United States, but problems of dependence lingered on to complicate Franco-American relations.

Wariness about the alliance continued throughout the period of the Confederation. It seemed to confer few benefits upon Americans. Commercial concessions in France that Jefferson had hoped might help to switch American trade from British to French channels were grudgingly granted and limited in scope and duration. When the new nation asked for French aid in opening the Mississippi River, which their Spanish ally had closed to American shipping, there was no response. Such aid as was offered to cope with the depredations of Barbary Pirates in the Mediterranean was not only ineffectual but raised the question whether the French were encouraging seizure of American ships to divert pirate attacks from their own vessels. And the old suspicions of the French conspiring with the British to ex-

[33] Robert Morris to Benjamin Franklin, Apr. 7 and July 1, 1782, Robert Morris Papers, Library of Congress.

clude Americans from the North Atlantic fisheries flourished. The upshot was that Americans believed with justification that France wished to keep them in a state of continuing dependence.[34] As the comte de Montmorin, Vergennes's successor as foreign minister, put it at the time the Constitution was being framed: "It suits France to have the United States remain in their present state, because if they should assume the consistence of which they are susceptible they would soon acquire a force and power which they would probably be very eager to abuse."[35]

In this circumstance it was understandable that the United States would broach the subject of terminating the alliance. The French responded negatively. While they placed little value on any American role in a future European war, they wished to minimize the chances of a reunification of the United States and Great Britain. Toward this end they preferred to see the British remain in possession of American northwest posts and Spain stirring Indian rebellion in the southwest.[36] Hence France's response to Jay's idea of considering the alliance inoperative was to berate the Americans for faithlessness and to profess astonishment at such a proposition. The king, according to Foreign Minister Montmorin in 1788, considered the alliance perpetual and inalterable.[37]

Such was the relationship between the two allies when

[34] See Frederick W. Marks, *Independence on Trial: Foreign Affairs and the Making of the Constitution* (Baton Rouge, La., 1973), pp. 106–7.

[35] Quoted ibid., p. 109.

[36] Alexander DeConde, *Entangling Alliance: Politics and Diplomacy under George Washington* (Durham, N.C., 1958), p. 11.

[37] Montmorin to Moustier, Archives Etrangères, Correspondance Politique, Etats-Unis, vol. 33, June 23, 1788, in *American Historical Review* 8 (1903): 728–29.

the Federal Union came into being. In light of French hostility to change, it is hardly surprising that *The Federalist Papers* reflected fears of France as well as of Britain, denouncing each for wishing to divide and exploit a vulnerable small nation. The experience of a decade appeared to be summed up in *The Federalist* No. 4, wherein John Jay warned against splitting "into three or four independent and probably discordant republics, or confederacies, one inclining to Britain, another to France, and a third to Spain, and perhaps played off against each other by the other three." The French alliance is not specifically mentioned in this or in any other *Federalist* paper, but where it is implied it is done with the intention of exposing its dangers. As Jay wrote in *The Federalist* No. 5, "How many conquests did the Romans and others make in the character of allies, and what innovations did they under the same character introduce into the governments of those whom they pretended to protect?"[38] Similar—though less pointed—references to the French alliance appeared in the Convention debates. At best it was obvious, as Madison pointed out, that the French joined us because of "the national contending passions" of France and England.[39]

Difficult as the relations were during the decade of the Confederation, the experience of the Federalist decade that followed was worse. If the early years of the alliance had been marked by troubles flowing particularly from Article VIII, in which the United States could not disengage from war without the approval of France, the 1790s were marked by the implications of Article XI, pledging the United States to defend "the present

[38] *The Federalist, or the New Constitution*, introduction by Carl Van Doren (New York, 1945), pp. 21 and 26.

[39] Max Farrand, ed., *The Records of the Federal Convention of 1787*, 4 vols. (New Haven, 1911–37), 1:456.

possessions of the Crown of France in America."[40] The outbreak of war between France and Britain in 1793 did precisely what John Adams had feared ten years before would occur; it made the United States "a football between contending nations," as each belligerent sought to create "a French party and an English party."[41] Thomas Jefferson was tempted to identify the future of republicanism in America with the survival of the Revolution in France, while Alexander Hamilton found in Great Britain the defender of civilization against French barbarism as well as the source of American credit and commercial prosperity.

France did not succeed in entangling the United States in the war with Britain, but it was not for lack of trying. Edmond Charles Genêt, the young Girondist enthusiast, arrived in the spring of 1793 to exploit Francophilic sentiment inflamed by the French Revolution. While American troops and American arms were not wanted, the French hoped to set in motion an invasion of Louisiana from American bases, to store and sell captured British prizes in American ports, and, above all, to arm vessels in the United States for privateering on the high seas. These were the least of services, so the French professed, that one ally might do for another.

Secretary of State Jefferson battled unsuccessfully against a neutrality proclamation, and his friends in the Congress failed to stop legislation to uphold the executive action. The Jeffersonians could not even deliver the "fair neutrality" that would permit American commerce to supply France with its West Indian products according to the provisions of the treaty of amity and com-

[40] Miller, *Treaties* 2:568–69.

[41] Butterfield, *Adams Diary and Autobiography,* Nov. 11, 1782, 3:51–52.

merce.[42] Genêt and his American friends had demanded the right to arm vessels in American harbors under Article XXIV of that treaty, only to be told by Jefferson that the treaty did not grant such a privilege. It simply denied the privilege to mutual enemies.[43] Pro-French newspapers, such as the *General Advertiser* of Philadelphia, railed against this strained and mean-spirited rendering of the treaties of 1778, claiming that the fitting out of ships of war was a right of France: "If the right is acknowledged to be given by the treaty of alliance, of consequence the permission of exercising that right is no breach of neutrality."[44] Hamilton wrote under a pseudonym to present a variety of objections, ranging from American inabilty to fulfill the conditions of the alliance to exemption from defending the West Indies on the ground that the alliance was defensive in principle and that the present war was offensive.[45] Hamiltonians won in 1793, and throughout the decade.

The Jeffersonians had not deserted the French cause; periodically during the 1790s they appeared to encourage a French conquest of England to save America from Hamiltonian monarchism. When the Jay Treaty in 1794 accommodated American policy to British interests by permitting British seizure of French goods on American ships, the Jeffersonians were outraged. When France broke relations with the United States over the Jay Treaty, insulted American commissioners abroad in the

[42] Jefferson to Madison, Apr. 28, 1793, Paul L. Ford, ed., *The Writings of Thomas Jefferson,* 10 vols. (New York, 1892–99), 6:232.

[43] Jefferson to Edmond Genêt, June 17, 1793, Andrew Lipscomb and Albert Bergh, eds., *The Writings of Thomas Jefferson,* 20 vols. (Washington, D.C., 1903–4), 9:131–37.

[44] *General Advertiser,* Philadelphia, July 11, 1793.

[45] Hamilton as "Pacificus" (June and July 1793), in Syrett, *Papers of Alexander Hamilton,* 15:xx and 33 ff.

XYZ affair, and committed depredations against American commerce, the Jeffersonians directed considerable anger at Federalist provocations of the French. They could empathize with France's sense of betrayal as the Washington and Adams administrations moved into the British orbit, and they admitted this behavior to have been a violation of the spirit if not the letter of the alliance.[46]

Yet the French misjudged the "French party" in America. What is most noteworthy about Francophile reaction in the Washington and Adams administrations was the Jeffersonians' relative unenthusiasm for action. They appeared self-defeating. If Hamilton won most of the battles of the 1790s, it may have been because the Jeffersonians could not take their gloves off. They wished for neutraliaty as much as and perhaps more than the Federalists. Their feelings for France were far less intense than their feelings against England.

The major energies of the Jeffersonians seemed to have been expended in preventing a Federalist alliance with England and consequent United States war with France. Whatever Francophilia survived in this campaign derived from fear of French anger over American behavior, an emotion that superseded concern for the fate of French republicanism among Jeffersonians, particularly since the Revolution by the end of the decade degenerated into despotism. Thus during the Quasi War with France in 1798 they worked unsuccessfully to prevent an American unilateral suspension of the alliance. Albert Gallatin argued that Congress lacked the power to perform such an act. And even if it had the authority, the treaty of amity and commerce, not the treaty of alliance, had been violated. Should the

[46] Lawrence S. Kaplan, "Toward Isolationism: The Rise and Fall of the Franco-American Alliance, 1775–1801," in Kaplan, *American Revolution,* p. 153.

issue turn on commercial wrongs, the Jay Treaty along with the French treaty should be equally denounced.[47] The *General Advertiser* took up this refrain and asked how any foreign country in the future could count on any treaty made with the United States.[48]

Most of the Jeffersonian arguments had nothing to do with loyalty to, respect for, or interest in the French alliance as such. Their concern was to avert a full breach with France out of fear of French revenge in the event of a British victory. Defending the French alliance was a temporary ploy to prevent a Federalist-British alliance. It worked. John Adams had no taste for the kind of British connection desired by his rival Hamilton. Even before the Quasi War reached its climax, Adams had asked his cabinet: "Will it not be soundest policy, even in case of declaration of war on both sides, between France and the United States, for us to be totally silent to England, and wait for her overtures? Will it not be imprudent in us to connect ourselves with Britain, in any manner that may impede us in embracing the first favorable moment or opportunity to make a separate peace? What aids or benefits can we expect from England by any stipulations with her, which her interest will not impel her to extend to us without any?"[49]

Granting the partisan intentions behind Washington's Farewell Address in 1796,[50] one may judge in light of

[47] *Annals of Congress,* 5th Cong., 2d sess., House of Representatives, July 6, 1798, p. 2126.

[48] *General Advertiser,* Philadelphia, July 4 and 7, 1798.

[49] John Adams to Heads of Departments, Jan. 27, 1798, in Charles Francis Adams, ed., *The Works of John Adams,* 10 vols. (Boston, 1853), 8:561–62.

[50] Alexander DeConde, "Washington's Farewell Address, the French Alliance, and the Election of 1796," *Mississippi Valley Historical Review* 43 (1957): 641–58.

the history of the Franco-American alliance that the president spoke for all. Jeffersonians might apply the strictures against "artificial ties" more readily to Britain, while Federalists would see a French alliance as more threatening. With the possible exception of some Hamiltonians, there was an American consensus that all alliances were both evil and dangerous and that the ensuing entanglement would place the interests of the United States at the service of a foreign power. Two American perceptions were operating here, one reinforcing the other. One of them rested on the assumption that larger, more powerful nations take advantage of alliances with smaller and weaker nations. The more important was that America, large or small, would be victimized by its connections with Europe.

American leaders, regardless of their political convictions, expressed the same sentiments on this subject, frequently in the same words. John Adams wrote in his diary in 1782: "It was easy to foresee that France and England both would endeavor to involve Us in their future Wars. I thought [it] our Interest and Duty to avoid [them] as much as possible and to be compleately independent and have nothing to do but in Commerce with either of them."[51] Less than a year later Madison in a congressional resolution against American adherence to the principles of the League of Armed Neutrals wrote that "the true interest of these states requires that they should be as little as possible entangled in the politics and controversies of European nations."[52] As Franco-American bitterness increased, John Quincy Adams agreed with his father that it was natural for a great state like France—and he could have included

---

[51] Butterfield, *Adams Diary and Autobiography*, Nov. 11, 1782, 3:52.

[52] Quoted in Irving Brant, *James Madison*, vol. 2, *James Madison, the Nationalist, 1780–1787* (Indianapolis, 1948), p. 206.

England as well—to intrigue with opposition parties in a small nation. This behavior "is founded deep in the human character, and all history is full of it."[53] Given the experiences with England and France, it is likely that Jefferson was wholly sincere when in his inaugural address he asked for "peace, commerce, and honest friendship with all nations, entangling alliances with none."[54] The Convention of Morfontaine in 1800 terminating the alliance of 1778 was signed by Adams and accepted by Jefferson—with relief by both men.

Repugnance for political connections with Europe became a vital part of the American isolationist tradition, a fundamental code that made alliances un-American propositions, even into the twentieth century. For 149 years no entangling alliance was made with any European nation. Then in 1949 the Truman administration challenged tradition to sign a treaty with eleven powers, including Britain and France—a treaty intended to last at least twenty years. The signing of an alliance, and of necessity an entangling alliance, was an act of courage.

That America was now the great power and France and Britain the lesser ones made little difference to critics such as Nettels, whose memories were fixed on the conditions as well as on the experience of the eighteenth century. A black American churchman, Bishop William J. Walls of the African Methodist Episcopal Zion Church, reminded senators of the Founding Fathers' trauma over Europe. By entering into the North Atlantic pact, the United States would be entangling itself with the very nations that were suppressing democratic impulses in their African colonies in the twen-

[53] John Quincy Adams to Abigail Adams, June 27, 1798, in Worthington C. Ford, ed., *Writings of John Quincy Adams*, 7 vols. (New York, 1913–17), 2:323–24.

[54] Richardson, *Messages and Papers of the Presidents*, 1:323.

tieth century just as they had done in America in the eighteenth century.[55] Another commentator, Alfred Kohlberg, spokesman for the American China Policy Association in 1949, could approve of the Atlantic pact as a step in the right direction if it were balanced by a Pacific pact. He was troubled, however, by "the breaking of a 152-year [*sic*] tradition of American foreign policy based on the Farewell Address of President Washington, who advised that we make no permanent alliances with European powers, but should rely on temporary alliances when needed."[56] H. M. Griffith, vice president of the National Economic Council, finally reached the conclusion many other critics of the North Atlantic Treaty were groping toward, namely, that if the United States should abandon its policy of abstaining from permanent alliances, "first commended by George Washington," it will "rescind the Declaration of Independence. American freedom of action will be gone. Surrender of freedom of action may well lead to our death as a Nation."[57]

Their message could not have been plainer. However disturbing the Soviet challenge might be for the moment, Europe had not changed; it was still the Continent that would corrupt virtuous America and ultimately drag it down to the destruction that would surely overtake Europe in the future. The image of American innocence was strong enough to withstand recognition on the part of isolationists that the United States of the twentieth century had been transformed from a small maritime nation into a giant, one of two superpowers which emerged from World War II.

It was this American Colossus that Europeans saw.

[55] "North Atlantic Treaty," *Hearings*, 3:1024–25.

[56] Ibid., p. 848.

[57] Ibid., p. 853.

American size and American strength seemed to be the only barrier against the onslaught of communism, whether from Communist parties within the West or from Russian pressures from the East. Only American wealth and generosity could rescue Europeans from the consequences of the physical destruction and psychic dysfunction caused by the war. But their very dependence upon the superpower of the West evoked emotions reminiscent of the character and tone of American reservations about their eighteenth-century alliance. Fundamentally, there was a suspicion that the United States, to place the words of Washington in a different context, "has a set of primary interests which to us have none or a very remote relation."[58]

Genuine as the common interest in the containment of communism may have been, the European allies suspected that they would function on a global stage as puppets manipulated by the American partner. Uneasiness over this prospect persists to this day, although its intensity has fluctuated over the thirty-year history of the Atlantic alliance. Its essence lay in the assumption that the strongest or predominant ally would dismiss the interests of the lesser members as expendable when its own interests were at stake.

Once the initial panic which had led them to accept the alliance had subsided, strains over their inferior status developed. These could never be fully quieted, and they helped to provide a negative gloss on every unilateral action of the United States. For example, the "hot line" between the White House and the Kremlin, designed to prevent such potential casus belli as the Cuban missile crisis or the Six-Day War in the Middle East, involved communications to which the smaller powers

---

[58] Washington, Farewell Address, in Richardson, *Messages and Papers of the Presidents*, 1:222.

were not privy even if their interests were involved. There was always the residual suspicion that acts were taking place over which they had no control but which would have important implications for their security. Even the idea of a balance of terror that grew out of apparent nuclear parity between the two great adversaries in the 1960s invited charges that American concern for Europe's safety had been sacrificed to its concern for the protection of its own cities. These charges in turn help to explain why Europeans were disturbed over the periodic discussion in the Congress over reduction or removal of American troops from European soil; the argument of savings in defense costs or the promotion of the spirit of disengagement did not suffice.

The conflict between the global scope of United States policy versus the continental emphasis of European allies was especially prominent in the Korean War of the 1950s and the Vietnam War of the 1960s and 1970s. In both wars the United States claimed that their firm response proved the credibility of their commitments to all alliances, including NATO. Europeans, however, read a different lesson from American actions: Korea diverted American power and energy better expended in Europe, while the apparent American obsession with the defense of South Vietnam raised doubts about the wisdom of American leadership in any part of the world.

Aside from the problem that a great power's interests might be irrelevant to its allies, there was the continuing difficulty of pressure on these nations to develop a defense capability they preferred to leave in the hands of the United States. The United States in the immediate post-Korean period forced its European allies to risk all the advances that had been made under the economic recovery program in order to prove themselves worthy of American military assistance. The Economic Cooperation Administration (ECA), which had carried out the Marshall Plan objectives between 1948 and 1951, gave way to the Mutual Security Program, in which economic aid was placed under a military rubric. When Senator Theodore A. Green was chairman of a Senate subcommittee investigating the state of European service to the alliance in 1951, he stated baldly that Europe had achieved its recovery under the Marshall program, and so "in the future economic aid is to be primarily for the purpose of assisting friendly countries to strengthen their individual and collective defenses. This is our main purpose in the United States. We find it necessary to give up plans for domestic economic development and to concentrate on building our defense. We expect our allies, within the limit of their capacities, to do no less."[59]

The ominous feature of this statement was the understanding that the United States would determine what was "within the limit of their capacities." Western Europe could envisage severe damage to a still precarious economic recovery as it faced inflation and the shortage of materials. Americans did not seem to appreciate that a strong economy could afford to serve both its domestic and military needs in ways weak economies could not manage.

American insensitivity also manifested itself to the NATO allies in the plans to defend Western Europe from a possible Soviet invasion. The projected battlefields would be in Europe, not in North America. Preparations for war meant preparations for fighting on their soil, and if this meant European acquiescence to

[59] Aug. 23, 1951, *Report* of the Subcommittee of the Committee on Foreign Relations on the United States Economic and Military Assistance to Free Europe (Green Subcommittee, "United States Foreign Aid Programs in Europe"), p. 22.

future American liberation of Europe, the allies would rebel. There was a casualness in the manner in which Americans talked of defense lines to be made on the Elbe, or on the Rhine, or even at the Pyrenees that frightened Europeans. Discussion in 1950 of a token defense on the Elbe with a major stand to be taken at the Rhine aroused the Dutch as well as the Germans.[60] This accusation of insensitivity against the American ally surfaced repeatedly in the 1950s, most notably after West Germany's entry into the alliance when the NATO war exercise Carte Blanche hypothecated a death toll of 1,700,000 people.[61] Such war games, even after they were revised, did little to alleviate suspicions among the lesser powers that the great power managed the alliance at their expense. The consequence of the frequent ruffling, conscious or unconscious, of national sensibilities was an anti-American mood among many of the allies. It rested on a conviction that the alliance was a trap with all the advantages on the side of the United States.

Of all the allies France has reacted against American suzerainty with greatest vigor, has expressed the deepest suspicions, and in short has behaved most like the United States of the eighteenth century. No country of Europe felt less secure in 1949 than France or was in greater need of external support. It was no coincidence that Georges Bidault, the French foreign minister in 1948, was one of the founding fathers of the Brussels Treaty, the forerunner of the North Atlantic Treaty. His intention was to lure the United States into the

[60] Konrad Adenauer, *Memoirs, 1945–53*, trans. Beate Ruhm von Oppen (Chicago, 1965), p. 267; Dirk U. Stikker, *Men of Responsibility: A Memoir* (New York, 1966), p. 297.

[61] Gordon A. Craig, "NATO and the New German Army," in William W. Kaufmann, ed., *Military Policy and National Security* (Princeton, 1956), pp. 221–23.

Brussels organization to exploit American power without having to sacrifice any European prerogatives.[62] The plan did not work as France had hoped. The United States did ultimately join the alliance but only after the successor treaty in 1949 had required, in Article III, assurance of "continuous and effective self-help" as well as "mutual aid."[63] France, and the other allies as well, worried about the terms of the mutuality. The price of American aid came high; it included base rights in Europe and an American role in internal affairs from the length of military service required of each nation's troops to recommendations of how much of a nation's gross national product should be dedicated to the alliance.

Analogies with the eighteenth century are striking. Just as French ministers in Philadelphia and French generals in the field exercised considerable influence through judicious distribution of blandishment and intimidation, along with appropriate funds, so well-staffed military assistance advisory groups wielded authority in Paris and other allied capitals. They demanded and received the rights and privileges of ambassadors. The American contingent in France was composed of eighty-eight Americans, while Norway was host to an American mission of sixty men, a bureaucracy larger than the entire Norwegian Foreign Office. The French were offended, but the most the Americans would do to appease their pride was to remove the patronizing term "advisory" from the title of the American military aid group in Paris.[64] Only then would the

[62] The intentions of Anglo-French diplomacy are clearly presented in *Foreign Relations of the United States* (hereafter *FRUS*), 1948, Western Europe, 3:1–16.

[63] "North Atlantic Treaty," *Hearings*, 1:2.

[64] Dec. 5, 1949, F. T. Greene Memo for General Lyman L. Lemnitzer, "Initial Discussion with the French of Bilateral MDAP Agree-

French sign the bilateral agreement legitimizing the American mission.

But the issue which evoked the sharpest Franco-American conflict was the American insistence on a German role in the Atlantic alliance. While communism was a serious problem for the French, the potential revival of German power was an even greater problem for them. Americans could not understand why they and Western European nations should provide the resources and manpower to protect German territory when Germans themselves did nothing to serve the common cause. Congress required that American aid be tied to self-help and mutual aid, and both these elements pointed to a German contribution in the form of soldiers. To many Americans the matter was as simple as that. To Frenchmen, however, memories of German bestiality under the Nazis half a decade before made it impossible for them to accept Germans as colleagues in a common effort. Lacking the experience of German occupation, American leaders could not fully comprehend the reasons why Frenchmen and other Europeans might shun German help even when such help would compensate for their own inadequate defense efforts.[65]

In the short run the result was the submission of France to American importunities by appearing to consent in 1951 to a German component in a European army. Here was a clearcut case of a senior partner forcing a junior partner to accept an unpalatable decision. The alternative could have been American abandonment of Europe, and perhaps European abandonment of France.

ment," Military Archives, Modern Military Branch, National Archives; Dec. 3, 1949, Ambassador in France to Secretary of State, No. 5106, *FRUS*, 1949, 4:681.

[65] See Laurence W. Martin, "The American Decision to Rearm Germany," in Harold Stein, ed., *American Civil-Military Decisions: A Book of Case Studies* (Birmingham, Ala., 1963), p. 646.

The humiliating experience of having to come up with a Pleven Plan (named for the French premier in October 1950) and of having to accept a European Defense Community (EDC) was not forgotten. The French nourished their grievances over the years and expressed them in a variety of forms, including the sabotage of the EDC in 1954, the aborted Suez invasion of 1956, and even formal withdrawal from the military functions of NATO in 1966. When the EDC failed, the United States threatened an anti-French alliance with Germany; when the British and French undertook an attack on Egypt without the knowledge of the American ally, the United States joined forces with the Soviet Union, or so it seemed, to foil the enterprise. As Marbois was reputed to have told Americans when they entered into an engagement with the common enemy behind France's back, great powers *"felt & remembered."*[66] Unlike the French in 1782, the United States also complained in 1954 and 1956.

Throughout this essay thus far the presentation of Franco-American relations in the course of two alliances has documented the assumption that small powers are victimized in the entanglement with a large power. For Americans during the Revolution this conclusion was especially significant because it reinforced an already pervasive belief that political connections of any sort with any European nation, large or small, were inimical to their interest, even to their survival. Embedded in American consciousness, the isolationist tradition remained virulent even when the United States had grown into the status France or England had earlier enjoyed; and yet many isolationist critics of the Atlantic pact spoke as if neither the United States nor Europe

[66] Notes on Debates, Mar. 15, 1783, Hutchinson, *Madison Papers,* 6:329.

had changed over 150 years. If America was no longer small, in their view it was still innocent and susceptible to the corruption of Europe.

Yet it is a moot point that the great power invariably exploits the small in an alliance. The latter possesses an ability to manipulate a relationship by virtue of its vulnerability. The long-term advantages may well fall to the lesser rather than to the greater partner in the alliance. Machiavelli suggested that when a state gives money to an inferior estate, "she gives an important sign of weakness." [67] Or, as Charles Burton Marshall translated this dictum, "Once we make another state the beneficiary of our aid, we tend in some degree to invest prestige in it. If the receiving state has marked political weaknesses, our giving of aid tends to plight us to the correction of its weaknesses." [68] The end result may be that the client regime has made its weakness an instrument of coercion against the benefactor.

Economists Mancur Olson and Richard Zeckhauser have noted that larger nations in alliances devote larger percentages of their total income to the common venture than do smaller nations. [69] While the senior partners may be annoyed over this disparity and prod the inferior allies from time to time about their irresponsibility, they should regard their share of the cost as reasonable and as a natural consequence of the conjunction of large and small nations. According to Olson and Zeckhauser, the greater powers place a higher absolute

[67] Niccolò Machiavelli, "Discourse on the First Decade of Titus Livius," in *Machiavelli: The Chief Works and Others,* trans. Allan Gilbert, 3 vols. (Durham, N.C., 1965), 1:409.

[68] Charles Burton Marshall, "Alliances with Fledgling States," in Arnold Wolfers, ed., *Alliance Policy in the Cold War* (Baltimore, 1959), pp. 219–20.

[69] "An Economic Theory of Alliances," *Review of Economics and Statistics* 47 (1966): 266–79.

value on the rewards of alliance and presumably have more money to spare than the lesser ones. The latter, having a smaller stake in the outcome, are potential prey to neutralism and tempted to make their own deals with the enemy. Moreover, they feel rightly that however great their sacrifice might be, it would have relatively small effect on the global balance. Should the major allies be inclined to withhold their aid, they often believe they would have more to lose than the beneficiary power. Therefore, the disproportionate sacrifice fits the circumstances of the alliance.

The Atlantic alliance provides dramatic illustrations of this thesis. If the term *entanglement* is meaningful, it should also apply to the way in which Western Europe entrapped the United States on the Continent after World War II on the grounds that the future of America hung on the fate of that region. Article V of the Treaty of Washington did not specifically require the United States to defend Europe in the event of attack, but it was understood on both sides that the language of that article, in which "the Parties agree that an armed attack against one or more of them in Europe or North America shall be considered an attack against them all," served that very purpose.[70] Knowledge that an attack on Paris would be treated as an attack on New York was the source of whatever sense of security the treaty offered Europeans in 1949.

When the Korean War converted the treaty into an active military organization Europeans demanded and Americans granted them (with some trepidation) a permanent American military force stationed in Europe in order to maintain the credibility of deterrence. This was the product of the New York and Brussels meetings of the North Atlantic Council in September and December

[70] "North Atlantic Treaty," *Hearings*, 1:2.

1950; and it was the occasion for a "Great Debate" in the Congress in 1951 over the president's authority to dispatch troops to Europe.[71] Although the United States asked in turn greater European military contributions and a commitment to a German share in the defense of Europe, it is important to observe that the American part of the bargain was fulfilled more effectively and more quickly than the European. France was able to withstand pressures from all sides as it delayed German entry into a European community because it knew that the United States set a high value upon its membership in the alliance, at least in the 1950s, and that no American retribution would follow from its resistance.

The permanent presence of American soldiers in the territories of allies offered a classic opportunity for the greater power to demonstrate its strength. Against the natural complaint of the host country that Americans committing crimes against its citizens on its soil should be tried in the civil courts of the country, the United States attempted to retain jurisdiction by means of its court-martial system. The allies protested. Americans would be in the position of an occupying power if its forces were exempted from domestic law. The Truman administration admitted the justice of the allies' complaints and feared consequences to the alliance should it not comply. Hence, the Status of Forces Agreement, signed in 1951 and ratified by the Senate in 1953, allowed Europeans criminal jurisdiction over Americans who broke the laws of their countries.[72] It

[71] See "Assignment of Ground Forces of the United States to Duty in the European Area," *Hearings,* U.S. Senate Committee on Foreign Relations and the Committee on Armed Services, 82d Cong. 1st sess., on S. Con. Res. 8, Feb. 1951.

[72] A full review of the background of the status-of-forces agreements is in Deputy Under Secretary of State Robert Murphy's testi-

was a difficult decision, since it invited a sustained attack upon both the Truman and Eisenhower administrations by isolationists in the Congress, led by Senator John Bricker of Ohio. The Bricker Reservation allowing each party to the treaty exclusive jurisdiction over its own forces rested on the emotional grounds that under the agreement American boys would lose their birthright, the protection of the Constitution through trial by jury.[73] Despite the isolationist clamor, the United States accepted the Status of Forces Agreement. There was no choice; the weaker powers might have abandoned the alliance over such a sensitive issue.

As for American global politics entangling Europeans in matters outside their interest and against their wills, the history of the Korean and Vietnam wars fails to sustain most of the charge. British Prime Minister Clement Attlee did fly to Washington in 1950 to restrain President Truman from employing atomic weapons in Korea and—sotto voce—to restrain General MacArthur from managing the war singlehandedly.[74] He succeeded in his mission, or at least in part of it. NATO's presence in the war turned out to be minimal. The United Nations force was essentially American, while the allies provided token support. On Vietnam their disapproval was open and articulate at a time when the United States had taken a firm stand that the sur-

mony before the House Committee on Foreign Affairs on proposed revision of agreement, July 19, 1955, in U.S. Department of State, *American Foreign Policy, 1950–55*, Basic Documents Publication 6446 (1955), pp. 1582–83.

[73] See U.S., Congress, Senate, Committee on Foreign Relations, "Agreement Regarding Status of Forces of Parties of the North Atlantic Treaty," *Supplemental Hearings*, 83d Cong., 1st sess., June 24, 1953, pp. 2–3.

[74] Dean Acheson, *Present at the Creation: My Years in the State Department* (New York, 1969), pp. 478–79.

vival of the free world was at stake in Southeast Asia. Despite an agonizing experience suffered in Vietnam, with Britain and France keeping their distance, the United States launched no reprisals. Indeed, when Senator Mike Mansfield, the majority leader of the Senate, proposed periodically in the late 1960s that the United States troop level be reduced or that troops be removed from Europe, the administration invariably heeded the vigorous objections of the European allies.[75]

The Atlantic alliance was and is important to the United States, as its behavior has demonstrated in almost every crisis of confidence. That it is equally if not more important to the European partners has not been quite so evident. It is, however, a vital fact in the longevity of NATO. It has not been American coercion that explains its survival thirty years after its inception. The existence of the North Atlantic Treaty may have been designed to inhibit a threat of Soviet invasion that never really existed. But the demoralization of Europe, its pessimism over its future, and the disruptive activities of strong Communist parties in France and Italy were realities in 1949. The linking of America with Europe may be judged a major factor in the psychological revival of the West which sparked the economic miracles of the next generation.

The allies paid a minimal price for the security American arms brought them. When they were unhappy with particular American positions, as in the case of plans for atomic installations in Denmark or of Spanish entry into the organization, they could reject American proposals with impunity. The greatest of all challenges was France's departure from NATO in 1966 without renouncing the North Atlantic Treaty itself. DeGaulle was

---

[75] See *New York Times*, Jan. 11, 1968, 14:4; Oct. 19, 1969, 25:1; Dec. 2, 1969, 2:4.

able to enjoy such benefits as the treaty conferred without having to pay penalties presumably demanded by military obligations.

The advantages of the smaller ally were even more apparent in the results of the Treaty of Paris than they were in the Treaty of Washington. Vergennes appeared to have been as badly entangled in the thickets of France's Spanish connection as were the Americans. Not only did the French depend on Spain's fleet for the success of their war with Britain; they had counted on a more resolute American cooperation in the waging of the war. If one looks objectively at the course of hostilities after the French alliance of February 1778, one can sympathize with France's unhappiness over the slackening of American efforts, over the obvious American wish to let the French finish the fighting for them.

Whether France betrayed the United States through secret talks with Britain and Spain, as Jay and Adams claimed, is open to question. While American appetite for western territory was not shared by the ally, the foreign minister believed, even as he agreed to restrict the boundaries of the new nation, that he was fulfilling the terms of the treaty. The United States had never really occupied the trans-Appalachian lands and the record of American troops in Ohio or Kentucky was not such as to assure American sovereignty over that area on the basis of military conquest. While there was French insensitivity to American needs as well as irritation over American demands for fishery rights, Vergennes never objected to Americans gaining such rights as long as there was no infringement upon France's claims.[76] The French felt that they had fulfilled their promise of winning American independence. If there

[76] Orville T. Murphy, "The Comte de Vergennes, the Newfoundland Fisheries, and the Peace Negotiation of 1783: A Reconsideration," *Canadian Historical Review* 46 (1965): 41.

was waffling and secrecy in the process, they were products less of the great power's malevolence than of its inability to extricate itself from the British war without concessions. British naval strength in the Caribbean and Spanish insistence on an equivalence for Gibraltar allowed the French few alternatives.

Vergennes's policies envisaged the reduction of British power in order to refashion Britain into a French associate in the maintenance of the balance of power in Europe.[77] America was a pawn in this enterprise. But it was a pawn that could manipulate the king by threatening to take actions that would jeopardize not only the large financial investment made by France but also the purpose for which the French made the alliance. An American rapprochement with Britain would undo the entire logic of France's policy and unravel all its schemes.

However angry Vergennes or his colleagues may have been over the activities of the American peace commissioners, no punishment was meted out. In a dispatch to the chevalier de La Luzerne, France's minister to the United States, sent in December 1782, Vergennes prevented the French minister from expressing France's anger over the underhanded dealings with Britain: "You may speak of it not in the tone of complaint. I accuse no person; I blame no one, not even Dr. Franklin. He has yielded too easily to the bias of his colleagues, who do not pretend to recognize the rules of courtesy in regard to us."[78] Franklin had understood and exploited France's constraints. Small wonder then that in his famous interview with Vergennes he was not

[77] Jonathan R. Dull, *The French Navy and American Independence: A Study of Arms and Diplomacy, 1774–1787* (Princeton, 1975), pp. 10–11.

[78] Quoted in footnote 9, Notes on Debates, Mar. 12–15, 1783, Hutchinson, *Madison Papers*, 6:332.

intimidated by the French statesman's accusation of ingratitude. The smaller ally was able to play upon the greater ally's larger stake in the alliance to win acceptance for its unilateral action.

After the war the French ally was guilty of many of the attitudes that the Americans found so offensive. For ten years after the Peace of Paris the French wished to restrict American western ambitions, refused to open ports to America in the West Indies, and generally exhibited contentment over the ineffectiveness of America's government. Yet most of their actions were vague and ineffectual. The Constitution was framed and went into effect despite French misgivings; indeed, the nation was hardly aware of French hostility to the change. As for their refusal to liberalize the terms of Franco-American commerce, this was a matter of France's own internal convulsions as the nation moved toward revolution rather than a considered intention to reduce American economic strength. The French could not salvage their own economy, let alone help the struggling new nation to reorder its economic structure.

The French Revolution from 1793 to 1800 certainly exposed the United States to the serious dangers of entangling alliances. France's purpose was to make a satellite of the United States, much as she had done in the case of her European neighbors. Harrison Gray Otis, a Massachusetts Federalist, had a valid point in asserting that the imperialist French "have an eye upon a *Cis Appalachian* as well as upon a *Trans Appalachian* Republic."[79] His language was intended to remind readers of the Cisalpine Republic which the French conquerors had established in northern Italy in 1797. And the fraternity which France of the Girondists had of-

[79] Harrison Gray Otis to William Heath, Mar. 30, 1798, in Samuel Eliot Morison, *Harrison Gray Otis, 1765–1848: The Urbane Federalist* (Boston, 1969), p. 104.

fered the United States would have embroiled the nation in another war with Britain.

But how much of the danger was real? Most of the emotions churned up over the evils of France at the time of the XYZ affair were aroused by Federalists for use against their Jeffersonian domestic enemies. Was a French invasion of the United States a genuine problem when Britain ruled the waves? The call for armies appeared to many Americans, including President Adams, to be a means of increasing the influence of General Hamilton rather than repelling imminent attack during the Quasi War. If any invasion was possible at this time, it was an Anglo-American assault on Spanish America.[80]

Whatever grief and embarrassment the United States suffered from the French alliance in the 1790s had to be weighed against the restrictions on American freedom of action. The facts were that the United States signed a treaty favoring the ally's enemy, then renounced unilaterally the treaties of 1778 and engaged in a naval war with the ally between 1797 and 1800, all without crippling repercussions from the senior partner. Admittedly, the French recalled their envoy, refused to receive the American minister in Paris, interfered with the election of 1796, and shamelessly tried to bribe and threaten peace commissioners who were sent to repair the relationship. Moreover, they seized American properties and imprisoned American sailors in violation of treaty obligations. But it is likely that relations with France would have been much the same without an alliance. The United States was subjected to British control, economically and even militarily. The hostility of France would have followed from these circumstances in any event.

[80] See in particular Albert Hall Bowman, *The Struggle for Neutrality: Franco-American Diplomacy during the Federalist Era* (Knoxville, Tenn. 1974), p. 434.

By the time of Morfontaine the alliance had lost meaning for both parties. The Americans were happy to detach themselves from it formally in 1800, while Bonaparte's primary interest in it was to divert them from his plans for Louisiana and their plans for French indemnities for depredations against American commerce during the Quasi War.[81]

Yet cynicism about the later years of the alliance distorts its early significance. Between 1778 and 1783 the alliance worked for both allies and worked remarkably well for the lesser ally. France achieved what it sought initially from the connection: it pried America loose from the British Empire. It even won a foothold of sorts in the American psyche. No matter how ungrateful or suspicious Americans were, there was a residue of good will and special feelings for France which began at this time and which have occasionally burst forth since. If France's participation was a tragedy for France and a personal failure for Vergennes, it was probably more failure for Vergennes than tragedy for France. The French Revolution comes down in history more as triumph than tragedy.

On balance the smaller power entangled the larger in an alliance that served American interests far more than it served the French. Whether the same results will apply to the history of NATO remains to be seen.

---

[81] See in particular Arthur A. Richmond, "Napoleon and the Armed Neutrality of 1800: A Diplomatic Challenge to British Sea Power," *Royal Service Institution Journal* 104 (1959): 1–9.

Contributors

ALEXANDER DECONDE is Professor of History at the University of California, Santa Barbara. His various articles and books include a trilogy in America's early relations with France: *Entangling Alliance: Politics and Diplomacy under George Washington* (1958); *The Quasi-War: The Politics and Diplomacy of the Undeclared War with France, 1797–1801* (1966); and *This Affair of Louisiana* (1976). Recently he served as Editor in Chief of the *Encyclopedia of American Foreign Policy: Studies of the Principal Movements and Ideas* (3 vols., 1978) and is presently involved in an international comparative study of foreign policies.

JONATHAN R. DULL is an Assistant Editor of *The Papers of Benjamin Franklin*. His first book, *The French Navy and American Independence: A Study of Arms and Diplomacy, 1774–1787* was published in 1975. A second book, *Franklin the Diplomat: The French Mission of Benjamin Franklin,* is awaiting publisher's decision.

LAWRENCE S. KAPLAN is University Professor of History at Kent State University. His works include *Jefferson and France* (1967), *Colonies into Nation: American Diplomacy, 1763–1801,* (1972), and *The American Revolution and "A Candid World,"* ed. (1977). He is presently Director of the Center for NATO Studies at Kent State University and author of *A Community of Interests: NATO and the Military Assistance Program, 1948–1951* (1980).

DIPLOMACY AND REVOLUTION

ORVILLE T. MURPHY is Professor of History at the State University of New York at Buffalo. His research interests are 18th-century military history, 18th-century diplomatic history, and the teaching of history. Among his publications on these subjects are: "The Comte de Vergennes, the Newfoundland Fisheries, and the Peace Negotiations of 1783" (1965); "Du Pont de Nemours and the Anglo-French Commercial Treaty of 1786" (1966); "The French Professional Soldier's Opinions of the Militia of the American Revolution Army" (1969); "On the Study of Diplomatic History" (1965). Professor Murphy is currently completing a biography of Charles Gravier, comte de Vergennes.

WILLIAM C. STINCHCOMBE is Professor of History at Syracuse University, Syracuse, New York. His publications include *The American Revolution and the French Alliance* (1969), "The Diplomacy of the XYZ Affair" (1977), and various other articles on diplomacy of the late eighteenth century. He is also diplomatic editor of vol. 3 of *The Papers of John Marshall* (1979). Forthcoming is a monograph on the XYZ affair (1980). Professor Stinchcombe's current research deals with democratic impulses in the 1790s.

Index

INDEX

Choiseul, Etienne François, duc de, 92, 110; secretary of state for foreign affairs, 2, 9, 79, 127–28
Choiseul-Praslin, duc de, 92
Clinton, Gen. Henry, 58
Codman, Richard, 69
Collins, Isaac, 51
Committee of Secret Correspondence, 3, 160
Common Sense, 40, 157–58; *see also* Paine, Thomas
Communism, containment of, 178
Continental Congress, 3, 5, 42, 58; and American military strength, 136–45; and birth of dauphin, 59–60; and Franco-American alliance, 6, 17, 39–40; and peace negotiations, 21, 59
Convention of 1800, *see* Morfontaine, Convention of
Cooper, Samuel, 65–66
Cornwallis, Gen. Charles, 18–19
Corsica, 81
Corwin, Edward S., 9, 26
Crèvecoeur, Hector St. John de, 156
Crimean crisis, 102–3, 105
Cuban missile crisis, 178

Dauphin, birth of, 56; birth, announcement of, 58–60; birth, celebration of, 43, 56–68
Deane, Silas, 3, 39, 160–61
Declaration of Independence, 5, 39–40, 156
De Gaulle, Charles, 189–90
Dickinson, John, 13
Digby, Adm. Robert, 58–59
Doniol, Henri, 10
Drinker, Elizabeth, 50
Duffield, Chaplain, 53
Dull, Jonathan R., 17, 21, 118
Dwight, Timothy, 55

Economic Cooperation Administration (ECA), 180
Estaing, Admiral d', 44, 77, 101, 132

European Defense Community (EDC), 184

Farewell Address, 31–33, 152, 174
Faÿ, Bernard, 11
Federalist Papers, 170
Federalists, 29–34, 173
Fisheries, North Atlantic, 22, 169
Fleury, Cardinal, 83, 117
Fleury, Colonel de, 140
Fleury, Joly de, 101
Floridablanca, conde de, 96
Fox, Charles James, 57–58
France, intervention in American Revolution, consequences, 74–78, 104–6
Franco-American alliance, 121, 125, 153–54, 161–62; origins, 2–17, 39, 96, 159–61; provisions, 7–8; relation to peace negotiations, 20–26, 163–67; after 1783, 26–35, 167–76; historiography, 1–37
Franco-Austrian Alliance of 1756, 82, 122
Franco-Russian Treaty of 1944, 152
Franklin, Benjamin, 3, 6–7, 19, 142; commissioner to Canada, 42–43; and Franco-American alliance, 14–15, 26, 39, 96, 160–61; peace commissioner, 24–25, 58, 164–65, 191
Frederick of Prussia, 113
French Revolution, 28, 75, 77, 105, 192

Gaine, Hugh, 54
Gallatin, Albert, 173
Garnier, 128
Gates, Gen. Horatio, 6
Genêt, Edmond C., 30, 171–72
George III of Great Britain, 58, 121
Gérard, Conrad Alexandre, 14–15, 128, 131–32, 134–36, 138–40
Germain, Lord, 98
Germantown, Battle of, 90, 131
Gibraltar, 21, 25, 101, 164
Gilbert, Felix, 13, 157
Grasse, Admiral de, 47, 100

INDEX